CONTEMPORARY FILM & the New Generation

Books in the YOUTH WORLD Series

CONTEMPORARY FILM & THE *NEW* GENERATION

PEACE, WAR & YOUTH

POPULAR SONG & YOUTH TODAY

CONTEMPORARY FILM & the New Generation

Edited by

LOUIS M. SAVARY
J. PAUL CARRICO

ASSOCIATION PRESS
New York

Contemporary Film & the *New* Generation

291 Broadway, New York, N.Y. 10007

Standard Book Number: 8096-1798-6

Library of Congress Catalog Card Number: 75-129429

Printed in the United States of America

Acknowledgments

Many of the works from which selections herein are taken are protected by copyright, and may not be reproduced in any form without the consent of the authors, their publishers, or their agents. Every effort has been made to trace the ownership of all selections in this book and to obtain the necessary authorization for their use. If any errors or omissions have occurred in this regard, corrections will be made in all future editions of this book. Since the copyright page cannot legibly accommodate all the acknowledgments and copyright notices, this page and the page following constitute an extension of the copyright page.

Grateful acknowledgment is made to: Atlantic-Little, Brown and Co. From *I Lost It at the Movies* by Pauline Kael, by permission of Atlantic-Little, Brown and Co. Permission granted for United States, the Philippines, Canada and the open market, copyright © 1954, 1955, 1961, 1962, 1963, 1964, 1965 by Pauline Kael; from *Kiss Kiss Bang Bang* by Pauline Kael, by permission of Atlantic-Little, Brown and Co. Permission granted for United States, the Philippines, Canada and the open market, copyright © 1965, 1966, 1967, 1968 by Pauline Kael. Bantam Books, Inc. from *Butch Cassidy and the Sundance Kid* by William Goldman. Copyright © 1969 by William Goldman. By permission of Bantam Books, Inc. All rights reserved. Fides Publishers, Inc. for selection by Anthony P. Schillaci from *Movies and Morals,* 1968. Harper & Row, Publishers for selection by Stanley Kauffman from *A World on Film,* 1966. Houghton Mifflin Company for selection by Philip Roth from *Goodbye, Columbus,* 1959. The Macmillan Company for selection by Ian Fleming from *Goldfinger,* 1966. William Morris Agency for selections by Robert Penn Warren from *Why Do We Read Fiction?* Used by permission. William Morrow and Co., Inc. From *MASH* by Richard Hooker. Reprinted by permission of William Morrow and Company, Inc. Copyright © 1968 by William Morrow and Company, Inc. The New American Library, Inc. From *Easy Rider* by Peter Fonda, Dennis Hopper and Terry Southern. Copyright © 1969 by Raybert Productions, Inc. Reprinted by arrangement with The New American Library, Inc. New York. Simon & Schuster, Inc. for selection by James Leo Herlihy from *Midnight Cowboy,* copyright © 1965 by James Leo Herlihy. Used by permission. The World Publishing Company. Reprinted by permission of The World Publishing Company from *The Graduate* by Charles Webb. An NAL book. Copyright © 1963 by Charles Webb.

Acknowledgment is gratefully made to the following newspapers, periodicals and magazines: *America* for selection by Michael Callahan. *Chicago Sun-Times* for selection by Roger Ebert. *Mademoiselle* for selections by Andrew Sarris. Used by permision of the author. *Media and Methods* for selection by Ned Hoopes. *New York Magazine* for selection by Judith Crist. *The New York Times* for selection by Bosley Crowther. *Newsweek, Inc.* for portions of articles by Joseph Morgenstern, copyright Newsweek Inc. Used by permission of Newsweek, Inc. and the author; for selections by Paul D. Zimmerman. Used by permission of the author. *Saturday Review* for selections by Larry Cohen (*SR* 12/27/69). Used by permission of the author. A collection of essays on film by Mr. Cohen soon to be published by The McGraw-Hill Book Company; for selections by Hollis Alpert. Used by permission of the author. *See* for selection by Sal Giarrizzo. *Show* for selection by Marvin Butterfield. Used by permission of Show Magazine. *Time, Inc.* for selections by Richard Schickel from *Life*. Used by permission of the author and for *Time* reviews of the films "Easy Rider" (7/25/69), "True Grit" (8/8/69), "Woodstock" (4/13/70), "Z" (12/5/69) and the Time Essay on Woodstock (8/29/69) and the interview with the Fonda family. Reprinted by permission from *Time,* the Weekly News Magazine: Copyright Time Inc. 1969, 1970. *Vogue* for selection by Ingo Preminger.

Contents

Little Miss Broadway © 1938 by Twentieth Century-Fox Film Corporation.

Preface

"Hollywood is dead. Long live film. Pass it on."

Through the late show, young people have come to know Hollywood and the Hollywood era of lavish sets, of superstars, of Shirley Temple and Clark Gable. It was a world of glamour and illusion, with Busby Berkeley aquatic scenes full of chorus girls dog-paddling in close formation. This was the era of the choreographed street dance, the cast of thousands, the fully orchestrated cavalry charge; of Roman gladiators with Brooklyn accents, of heroines with thousand-dollar wardrobes playing $75-a-week secretaries.

The star-spangled escapist romances are not all on the late show. Lots of the same things still happen in schmaltzy ten-million-dollar nothing-new movies. In the '50's and '60's prime-time TV took over much of the territory formerly covered by B movies. TV offers plenty of soap opera, a sufficiency of situation comedies—known in the trade as "sitchcoms" or "sitcoms," and ranging in quality from poor to bad to wretched. The formula Westerns have mostly moved to the small screen now. The TV carries the bulk of the spy-adventure-police dramas (some of them good) that were at one time the exclusive province of the movies.

But in the last few years, in movieland, other work has been done, and films have started to open up a bit. Film history must now record the fact that the stories have been told of the slow-motion machine-gun killing of two gangster lovers; of a midnight cowboy and a crippled bum under the neon of Times Square; of some freewheeling, wisecracking army surgeons patching bloody bodies near the Korean front; of the easy journey across the country and into death of two young motorcyclists; of a flower child judged unfit for military service because his record shows he was arrested for littering. Film in America, and film in the world, will never be the same. "You can't go home again." No longer content to fashion a world apart, a silver screen world, young, and even older, filmmakers are searching on behalf of young audiences for images of the real world as they see it.

In this book, the selections and stills from film scripts, the comments from directors, actors, producers, critics, and commentators–all center around the values and value-issues found in the films which engage the attention of today's box-office customers–the under thirties.

*M*A*S*H*. Courtesy of Twentieth Century-Fox Film Corporation.

Part 1

LOWBROW, HIGHBROW, MIDDLEBROW MOVIES:

FILM TODAY AND YESTERDAY

Movies are finally getting to where it is.
When they get where it really is,
the audience gets there to see it.
The kids know. . . .
Now that Easy Rider'*s making it,*
a lot of smart (maybe brilliant)
new film-makers will be able to
find out if they are brilliant.

Dennis Hopper

City Lights. Courtesy of United Artists Corporation.

First came the silents, then the talking pictures. And among them—in the '20's and '30's, then again in the '40's and '50's—there were really good movies that almost everybody liked. There was the magic of Chaplin's films, for instance, which evoked the elf and the clown and the fool inside Everyman.

As time passed, it became clear that many movies were badly made by tasteless producers for audiences presumed to be stupid. Also clear was the fact that there was room in this new medium for art as well as hackwork. Many directors were merely good or bad foremen shuffling good or bad actors and actresses around in front of cameras. Some directors learned, however, that they could give a very personal stamp to the material they shot and edited.

> We made funny pictures as fast as we could for money. We knew we were experimenting with something new — but has there ever been a performer, or a creative person of any kind, from a talented potato peeler to Picasso, who didn't think he was original? But we didn't rear back and publish manifestoes like the modern poets and painters nobody can understand. All the philosophizing and the explaining and the phrases with lace on them, like "cineplastic art," came much later.
>
> Mack Sennett

In Europe and in America a race of critics rose up alongside tribes of newly expert viewers. As more people got to know more about movies, comparisons were made, opinions were formed. There were directors, cameramen, choreographers, writers, scenarists, and actors and actresses who began to achieve reputations for being good at what they were doing for a living—some of them very good.

In a few cases, critics became directors. As directors they insisted upon doing what a few had done from the beginning–writing their own scripts, doing their own casting, making their own choices about what to put in or leave out. Godard, Truffaut, Fellini and Bergman came into prominence as directorial superstars. They often wrote for their own audiences, though sometimes their definition of the audience was a little vague. For instance, in an interview with Jean-Luc Godard, we find the following:

Interviewer: "Do you make films for the audience or an audience?"
Godard: "For the audience, of course."
Interviewer: "What audience?"
Godard: "The right audience."

As movies grew up the cult of filmmaking grew up, and a kind of High–Church, or at least highbrow, audience developed, a kind of self-appointed priesthood that not only read subtitles but could compare hidden meanings and talk intelligently about styles and sort out the eternal and everlasting from the earthbound and cinematically sinful. And with the priesthood came a kind of religion of the art-house crowd who scorned the less expert moviegoers and the movies *they* thought were good.

Who were the other moviegoers? The middlebrows, who were not totally at the mercy of Hollywood, and the lowbrows, who accepted more or less everything offered them. The lowbrows were the mom and pop types and their sons and daughters of the kiddie matinees who marched uncritically off to see Bobby Breen in the '30's and B-grade John Wayne in the '40's and Doris Day in the '50's and Vincent Price in the '60's. They could be the moms and pops and sons and daughters of the poor or middle or even upper classes. But they'd see whatever the local moviehouse served along with the popcorn.

Then there were the middlebrows, those customers of every socioeconomic class whose education—film and otherwise—had prepared them to be a little more choosy. They wouldn't go to see the really bad films, but you'd never get them into a theater that showed an Italian film . . . unless it were very well advertised. They might buy *La Dolce Vita* but they wouldn't take *8½*. They liked a good story. They were *Cactus Flower* or *True Grit* people, who'd like *The Apartment* but not *The Adventurers,* who'd enjoy *Tom Jones* but not *Wild Strawberries* or *Persona.*

Persona. Courtesy of Marc Gervais.

Dr. Zhivago. Courtesy of Marc Gervais.

Of course, judgments about movies have always been complicated, because people react in different ways to different films. A routine film might be watched by highbrows because of an expert cameraman's work in it. Lowbrows might develop an interest in a star, and learn to notice many differences in the films the star is in. Or a terrible director might fascinate certain groups just because he is so bad.

But what the young movie audiences today are doing is splitting from this scene entirely . . . or almost so. They are partly "post-brow," and maybe partly "no-brow," in the sense that they can be fairly objective, without the pretense of the art-house crowd. They get trapped into seeing bad stuff, of course. Like anyone else they get confused by the promotion and advertising. But they get smarter faster, because they see more and know more.

The young audiences will sit through the odd good comedy or drama. But they won't settle for a steady diet of good, unspectacular, well-made films, like *Funny Girl* or *Dr. Zhivago* or *Promise at Dawn* or *Ryan's Daughter*. They've seen a few foreign films—maybe more than a few. Many of them have taken courses in film or have been exposed in school to a variety of good films—long ones and short ones, Canadian documentaries and Bergman classics. They aren't snobs. Nor do they need foreign films because (though it used to be true) seeing French or Italian or Czech movies is a way to see nudity with some art, rather than nudity without art, as in the American skin flicks. But nudity is normal now, and foreign films are no longer necessarily artier than American movies. The young audiences are ready for something besides Godard, something besides Bergman, something not encountered but partly prepared for by the earlier, highbrow art-house crowd.

The long lines of young people are forming for another purpose. They are looking for another kind of experience. What is it they want to see? Not uninspired stuff, not merely OK stuff, and not just any old foreign film. Benjamin Braddock who was offered "Plastics!" didn't want any. And it was just about the time of Benjamin Braddock's graduation party that the new classics began to appear. . . .

Who Is the Audience?

According to certain estimates more than 70 per cent of today's movie audiences are between the ages of 16 and 29. This realization struck the film industry as it was watching the figures come in on revenue from *The Graduate*. So naturally today more and more films are being made with the young audience in mind.

The Sixties

In reviewing the '60's, one finds a clue as to why certain types of films are being made, why tastes are changing and improving, and why the movie industry has lost its security. This is by no means a thorough investigation of influences, trends and accomplishments, but is merely a peek at the evolution which has taken place . . .

Young people have helped shape the destinies of Hollywood's movie moguls, producers, directors and actors. They have embraced the personal statement film and have rejected the "lowest common denominator" film. But in order to examine a bit closer the changing trends, one must turn to the

"Interim Generation," the people who were teenagers during the silent fifties, for a wider screen view. This was the midi-McLuhan generation, with television being introduced to them in their pre-teen years. By the time they graduated from high school, many of them were sick of TV and tired of the same type of movies. So, while in college, they began to embrace the foreign films. As the fifties were coming to a close, it was more than just intellectually chic to see a Fellini, Bergman or Kurosawa film. A whole new audience, semi-visually literate, had been created out of the despair of mediocrity. Art houses began creeping up all over the country and Hollywood began to take notice. Foreigners such as Simone Signoret, Sophia Loren and Lila Kedrova even won Oscars.

During the sixties, other imaginative foreign directors made their mark on cinema. Besides the aforementioned patron saints, the sixties saw the meteoric rise of Truffaut, Antonioni, Godard and others. It would be fallacious to maintain that these directors are sure-fire box office. Many still play to very limited audiences. But others do not, and their over-all influences on the movie industry and audiences cannot be underestimated.

While the awareness and appreciation of foreign films has continued to grow through the sixties, the vast majority of even the under-thirty clique still patronizes American films more. But the success of the Truffauts, Widerbergs and Lelouches has made it possible for the creative film directors in the U. S. to do their own thing.

Blow-up. Courtesy of Marc Gervais.

So from the banality of the '50's in American films, the past decade saw the emergence of the personal statement film, the experimenters and the movie polemicists. The torch was passed from Elia Kazan, George Stevens and Stanley Kramer to Arthur Penn, Stanley Kubrick, Mike Nichols, et al. Not that this type of film was nonexistent before. One could not exclude fine films like *On The Waterfront, Giant* and *The Defiant Ones*. But they were exceptions and weren't trend setters. Also they were not innovative cinematically, even though they did deal with social problems. Technically, *Waterfront* did not differ much in 1954 from a truly innovative film, *Citizen Kane,* which was made in 1939. Nor did the directors of these films continue to grow, challenge the Hollywood establishment or experiment. Whereas a Stanley Kubrick did; consider *Lolita* (1962), *Dr. Strangelove* (1964) and *2001: A Space Odyssey* (1968).

The real turning point came in 1967 with the monumental successes of *Bonnie and Clyde* and *The Graduate*. For not only did these films enjoy colossal remuneration despite the fact that none of the actors was established box-office potential, but in embracing these movies, the young film-goer supported films of high artistic achievement which experimented with the medium. They know and want quality and when the cash register jingles for quality, Hollywood listens . . .

The cheapie films made expressly for the teen market, i.e., the beach party flicks, motorcycle and sado-sex party films have dissipated (consider the

Dr. Strangelove. Courtesy of Museum of Modern Art.

evolution from *Hell's Angels on Wheels* to *Easy Rider*; some cycle!). Even more intriguing is that the profusion of sex-ploitation films is not attracting the young crowd but rather the "silent majority."

SAL GIARRIZZO
See Magazine

A scene from *Bob and Carol and Ted and Alice,* a Frankovich Production from Columbia Pictures. Copyright © 1969 Columbia Pictures.

Books vs. films

The young audience for books has not so much shrunk as the young audience for motion pictures has appreciably grown and become more vocal . . .

In the process of this shift of focus off the writer and onto the film-maker, the literary gods lost many of their aspiring novices to a medium that was itself in a state of relative infancy.

If *Blow-Up* was instrumental in attracting young people to film, the equivalent American landmark was Mike Nichols's *The Graduate.* Holden Caulfield, his worried future, identity-crisis, and traumas fairly intact, found a close screen ally in the person of Benjamin Braddock as played by Dustin Hoffman. Both characters assert the same basic appeal, a nervy and youthful cry against hypocrisy and false values that are captured lucidly by one word: *plastics.* What seems to me to be vital about the movie is that it signifies a phenomenon of rapport rather than a purely esthetic triumph; that it functions as a sociological replacement for Salinger despite its own confusions and impurities of self-conscious camerawork; that its score is by Simon and Garfunkel rather than Max Steiner.

This alliance with contemporary music has a great deal to do with the new look of American films and their success with a young audience. The Grateful Dead, Big Brother and the Holding Company, and John Barry's superb orchestrations contributed heavily to the impact of *Petulia.* And the two international or coincidental imitations of Nichols's films —*Goodbye, Columbus* and *I Love You, Alice B. Toklas*—respectively used the Association and Harper's Bizarre for their title songs. When the team responsible for writing the latter movie made their directing debut this year with *Bob & Carol & Ted & Alice,* they appropriately ended what is in essence a middle-aged comedy with Dionne Warwick singing "What the World Needs Now Is Love."

LARRY COHEN
Saturday Review

2001: A Space Odyssey

In the late '60's Stanley Kubrick's *2001: A Space Odyssey* was to divide the critics—most of whom are over thirty—right down the middle. The reactions of the movie generation, which grew up with TV, were to prove perceptive.

A fan letter

DEAR MR. KUBRICK:

I'm 15½ years old, going into my junior year at John Browne High School in Flushing, and am what is commonly referred to as a movie nut. But the picture I'm most nuts about is your unprecedented masterpiece, *2001: A Space Odyssey*. I saw it for my first time at the Loew's Capitol Theater in New York, and was thoroughly spellbound by the picture I had waited for for three years. I went back to see it again with my brother, who is in the Air Force, and he will see it again with one of his buddies next week in Washington, D.C., where he is stationed. Since then, I have written a review of *2001* (highly complimentary, of course), which drew raves from my English teacher and will probably be printed in the school social studies magazine next September. I have bought the souvenir book, the soundtrack album, the personality poster advertisement, and have scores of advertisements from magazines and newspapers. I keep a record of reviews that *2001* has received, mostly from New York publications. I am happy to announce that 33 are excellent, which is much more than the reviews that were not so good. The unfairest review I have seen yet is Kathleen Carroll's atrocity in the *New York Daily News*. I'm thoroughly convinced she has absolutely no idea what she's talking about, and I sometimes wonder if she ever *saw* the film. I also keep a record of how much money *2001* makes by reading *Variety* every week. Of course, it does not list every theater the picture is playing at, but from the looks of business from the theaters it does list, *2001* is doing, in *Variety* terms, boffo biz. I intend to see the film at least twice more, and take my father and mother with me, because I'm sure it would be a totally new experience for them. I myself have thought of becoming a film director, and if you could possibly find any time in your busy schedule, do you think you could write me a short letter giving me some tips on how to get started in the business? Before I saw *2001* I wrote two other famous directors, but I did not receive a reply from either of them, probably because of their busy schedules. Enclosed is a copy of my review, which I hope you will find enjoyable. I'm not Bosley Crowther, but I do the best I can. Thank you very much for allowing me to use up so much of your time, but I felt I had to write the man whom I consider my idol, and to let him know that I'm just one of many who consider this man the best, most inventive director in the film industry.

MICHAEL SINGER
Flushing, New York

2001: A Space Odyssey. Courtesy of MGM Pictures.

Also in favor

DEAR MR. KUBRICK:

I am a senior at Radcliffe College, majoring in English. *2001* was WOW, FUN, KEEN, NEAT! Congratulations.

JODY ADAMS
Cambridge, Massachusetts

P.S. *Dr. Strangelove* was great, too.

DEAR MR. KUBRICK:

I am three and one-half years old.
You're right!

[Name withheld on parents' request]
Champlain, New York

DEAR MR. KUBRICK:

I know you must think a boy, 14 years old, must be crazy to write a letter to a big producer such as you, but I had to express my thoughts about your recent film. I thought it was great! It's about time somebody made a film about the true science fiction of today. After a while, you get sick of seeing nothing but giant monsters from outer space. It was great. It's been seven weeks since I saw your movie, and I remember the film as well as I know the hangnails on my fingers. Course you know what the critics said. Well, I say down with the critics. They're about as dependable as the Nielsen ratings on television. I thought *2001* was the best film I've seen in the past three years.

KIM ELLISON
Hayward, California

DEAR MR. KUBRICK:

My pupils are still dilated, and my breathing sounds like your soundtrack. I don't know if this poor brain will survive another work of the magnitude of *2001*, but it will die (perhaps more accurately "go nova") happily if given the opportunity. Whenever anybody asks me for a description of the movie, I tell them that it is, in sequential order: Anthropological, camp, McLuhan, cybernetic, psychedelic, religious. That shakes them up a lot.

Jesus, man, where did you get that incredibly good technical advice and information? Whenever I see the sun behind a round sign, I start whistling *Thus Spake Zarathustra*. My kettledrum impression draws the strangest looks.

ROBERT HIGGINS
Detroit

DEAR MR. KUBRICK:

Being young enough to look forward to 2001 as the prime of my life, I must thank you for giving me a glimpse of what terror and beauty may await us in that year.

BOB WRIGHT
Atlanta, Georgia

2001: A Space Odyssey. Courtesy of MGM Pictures.

2001: opposed

DEAR MR. KUBRICK:

I would have to say that, in all honesty, the advertising campaign that preceded this picture was, to say the least, *deceitful;* on my family's part, it was not that much of a let-down, because we were not one of the young children who were tricked into believing that this was a science-fiction epic, while all it was was a deep insight into the creation of the universe.

JULIAN J. NUSSBAUM
North Miami Beach, Florida

DEAR MR. KUBRICK:

I must tell you it is the worst picture I have ever seen. I have been racking my brain all afternoon trying to figure out the point you were trying to make, and it is beyond my understanding. I think you were trying to tell us something about life, but what it is, I just can't determine. My girl friend and I watched the audience's reaction as the people were leaving the theater. Some people stared at each other and said nothing, while others laughed. The movie made no sense to me at all. Never before in my 19 years have I left a movie knowing nothing what it was about. Perhaps I just haven't lived long enough to know very much about life, but I should have gotten something from this movie, but I was left with nothing.

THERESE KUSTRA
College Point, New York

Two reactions

The critic for *The Village Voice* assesses the young audience and its fascination for *2001.* In terms of their life experiences, they are much different from his generation.

> [Comparing *2001* and *Belle de Jour*]: I find that most of the young people who see *Belle de Jour,* people in my [university] classes for example, don't like it as much as they liked *2001: A Space Odyssey.* . . . I think there's a separation there in sensibilities between the young and old, and I think *Belle de Jour* is a film that would appeal to those who grew up with a certain measure of frustration in their lives and not to the people who've grown up with so much erotic affluence that they're bored by it. . . . I think perhaps Stanley Kubrick belongs to this generation, to the new generation in a certain way. And therefore, I think it is almost impossible to reconcile these two positions, to reconcile these two reactions–reaction to *Belle de Jour,* which I think is the best film of the year by far, and my reaction to *2001*.
>
> ANDREW SARRIS

2001: A Space Odyssey. Courtesy of MGM Pictures.

BONNIE AND CLYDE: Attack and counterattack

Today's audience is vocal in a non-unrealistic way about its films. In 1967 *Bonnie and Clyde* attracted as much critical and public controversy as Antonioni's *Blow-Up*. Bosley Crowther, then critic for *The New York Times,* attacked *Bonnie and Clyde* as "a cheap piece of bold-faced slapstick comedy that treats the hideous depredations of that sleazy, moronic pair as though they were as full of fun as the jazz-age cut-ups in *Thoroughly Modern Millie.*"

> The film is assembled in a helter-skelter fashion and played at an erratic, breakneck speed that oftentimes gives the brash succession of hold-ups, shootings and getaway chases in old-fashioned automobiles the appearance of Mack Sennett slapstick comedy. It whips through the saga of the cheapjack bandits as though it were funny instead of sordid and grim . . .
>
> Arthur Penn, the aggressive director, has evidently gone out of his way to splash the comedy holdups with smears of vivid blood as astonished people are machine-gunned. And he has staged the terminal scene of the ambuscading and killing of Barrow and Bonnie by a posse of policemen with as much noise and gore as is in the climax of "The St. Valentine's Day Massacre."
>
> This blending of farce with brutal killings is as pointless as it is lacking in taste, since it makes no valid commentary upon the already travestied truth. And it leaves an astonished critic wondering just what purpose Mr. Penn and Mr. Beatty think they serve with this strangely antique, sentimental claptrap.
>
> BOSLEY CROWTHER
> *The New York Times*

From the motion picture *Bonnie & Clyde* copyright © 1967 by Warner Bros. Pictures, Inc.

The Times' readers were quick to answer:

TO THE EDITOR:

I am sorry that *Bonnie and Clyde* does not impress Mr. Crowther as a contribution to the thinking of our times. I think the film is an outstanding statement of the frightened anguish of violence and of the great beauty and terror which life can comprehend. To a generation seeking to bring new and real meaning to life in a decade characterized by brutal, senseless violence, such a film is emphatically of special relevance.

STEPHEN M. EGE
Student, University of
Chicago Law School

From the motion picture *Bonnie & Clyde* copyright © 1967 by Warner Bros. Pictures, Inc.

TO THE EDITOR:

Surprisingly, Mr. Crowther has forgotten or perhaps ignored the elemental freedom of the artist to place his perspective and patterns on his material. Arthur Penn has not made an educational or historical filmstrip on the desperadoes of the thirties. He has used the framework of the Bonnie and Clyde legend as a comment on a society that relies on one more escalation of violence to put itself in the clear.

If Mr. Crowther denies Mr. Penn this freedom to create his personal vision, he must have run screaming from Luis Bunuel's *The Exterminating Angel.* Here, Bunuel has placed an arbitrary structure on his film that allows him to explore his favorite themes—the shallow rich and the Mother Church. If we were to be completely factual, we would merely laugh at the guests' failure to break from the room. Rather, we are intrigued and won.

On the other hand, Penn has deliberately played the first section of *Bonnie and Clyde* subjectively and lightly as the main characters and their milieu react to a life of crime as a child would react to a toy that releases him from a bout of crying. Those were hard times, when heroes were few, and Americans have always admired the man who could bust the bigwigs with style and get away with it. The film makes an intelligent comment, that only becomes evident in the second half, about America's heritage of crime and its penchant for violence, so evident today. What began as a jaunt for Bonnie and Clyde turns into a nightmare as their own blood starts flowing and not some crumpled policeman's. (As Bonnie says to Vilma, "It's not like you were the law. You're jes' folks, like us.") That is why the disgusting violence of Buck's death and Blanche's blinding and the morbidly repeated machine-gunnings of Bonnie and Clyde are so necessary. They are the brutal turnabout that gives the lie to the belief that violence will solve all your problems.

Faye Dunaway's starlet qualities add to the romantic aura of the first half. She makes the dream seem actually possible, only to be turned to ironic advantage later. However, the casting also allows Penn to diabolically turn the film on his audience (which has been lapping it all up) and prove his primary point—that violence can be applauded if it is suitably packaged and attractively put forth.

This extra dimension of insight into character, milieu and audience is what makes the film worth so much more than what Mr. Crowther will admit. For, in the end, Arthur Penn does not sympathize with Bonnie and Clyde as criminals but as human beings who have been duped by the mythical efficacy of violence.

JOSEPH H. O'MEALY
College of the Holy Cross, '70

"Exploiting the worst in us"

But Mr. Crowther also had his supporters, mainly from the older generation:

TO THE EDITOR:

Mr. Crowther will find support in his campaign against gratuitous violence in George Orwell's *1984*. In one of that clairvoyant book's most horrible passages, the brainwashed Winston Smith makes this diary entry:

"April 4, 1984. Last night to the flicks. All war films. One very good one of a ship full of refugees being bombed. . . . Audience much amused by shots of a great huge fat man trying to swim away with a helicopter after him . . . then he was full of holes and the sea around him turned pink . . . audience shouting with laughter when he sank" . . .

The passage from Orwell suggests to me at least that the most significant drama going on in the crowded movie houses is in front of the screen rather than on it. Our beady-eyed relish for stabbings, incinerations, dismemberment and slow strangulation has more to tell us about ourselves and about violence too than all the gore-splattered nonsense we pay so eagerly to see.

FREDERICK HIGHLAND
New York City

From the motion picture *Bonnie & Clyde* copyright © 1967 by Warner Bros. Pictures, Inc.

BONNIE AND CLYDE:
gangster violence

So *Bonnie and Clyde* was such a new departure from the gangster films of the past that the critics as well as the public were caught completely off guard. Many critics did not support the film at first, because of the violence and its treatment. Others reacted differently.

"The film of the '60's"

> The violence in most American movies is of a curiously bloodless quality. People are shot and they die, but they do not suffer. The murders are something to be gotten over with, so the audience will have its money's worth. The same is true of the sex. Both are like the toy in a Crackerjack box: Worthless, but you feel cheated if it's not there.
>
> In *Bonnie and Clyde,* however, real people die. Before they die they suffer, horribly. Before they suffer they laugh, and play checkers, and make love, or try to. These become people we know, and when they die it is not at all pleasant to be in the audience.
>
> ROGER EBERT
> *Chicago Sun-Times*

A critic changes his verdict

Letters to editors and loud arguments in homes and coffeehouses protested and defended *Bonnie and Clyde*. Sociologically it became the largest animated Rorschach test in America. The National Catholic Office for Motion Pictures commended it as the best film of the year while other groups called for its censure and censorship. Joseph Morgenstern, the *Newsweek* critic, at first wrote a negative review of the film, in which he took approximately the same stance toward the movie as Crowther. A week later he did something almost unheard of for a critic—he changed his mind:

> Last week this magazine said that *Bonnie and Clyde,* a tale of two young bank robbers in the 1930's, turns into a "squalid shoot-'em for the moron trade" because it does not know what to make of its own violence. I am sorry to say I consider that review grossly unfair and regrettably inaccurate. I am sorrier to say I wrote it.
>
> Seeing the film a second time and surrounded by an audience no more or less moronic than I, but enjoying itself almost to the point of rapture, I realized that *Bonnie and Clyde* knows perfectly well what to make of its violence, and makes a cogent statement with it—that violence is not necessarily perpetrated by shambling cavemen or quivering psychopaths but may also be the casual, easy expression of only slightly aberrated citizens, of jes' folks.
>
> I had become so surfeited and preoccupied by violence in daily life that my reaction was as excessive as the stimulus. There are indeed a few moments in which the gore goes too far, becomes stock shockery that invites standard revulsion. And yet, precisely because *Bonnie and Clyde* combines these gratuitous crudities with scene after scene of dazzling artistry, precisely because it has the power both to enthrall and appall, it is an ideal laboratory for the study of violence, a subject in which we are all matriculating these days.
>
> JOSEPH MORGENSTERN
> *Newsweek*

BONNIE AND CLYDE:
American folk heroes

Structurally, *Bonnie and Clyde* is a story of love on the run, like the old Clark Gable-Claudette Colbert *It Happened One Night,* but turned inside out; the walls of Jericho are psychological this time, but they fall anyway . . .

Bonnie and Clyde brings into the almost frighteningly public world of movies things that people have been feeling and saying and writing about. And once something is said or done on the screens of the world, once it has entered mass art, it can never again belong to a minority, never again be the private possession of an educated, or "knowing," group. But even for that group there is an excitement in hearing its own private thoughts expressed out loud and in seeing something of its own sensibility become part of our common culture.

Our best movies have always made entertainment out of the anti-heroism of American life; they bring to the surface what, in its newest forms and fashions, is always just below the surface. The romanticism in American movies lies in the cynical tough guy's independence; the sentimentality lies, traditionally, in the falsified finish when the anti-hero turns hero. In 1967, this kind of sentimentality wouldn't work with the audience, and *Bonnie and Clyde* substitutes sexual fulfillment for a change of heart. (This doesn't quite work, either; audiences sophisticated enough to enjoy a movie like this one are too sophisticated for the dramatic uplift of the triumph over impotence) . . .

Bonnie and Clyde needs violence; violence is its meaning. When, during a comically botched-up getaway, a man is shot in the face, the image is obviously based on one of the most famous sequences in Eisenstein's *Potemkin,* and the startled face is used the same way it was in *Potemkin*—to convey in an instant how someone who just happens to be in the wrong place at the wrong time, the irrelevant "innocent" bystander, can get it full in the face. And at that instant the meaning of Clyde Barrow's character changes; he's still a clown, but *we've* become the butt of the joke.

It is a kind of violence that says something to us; it is something that movies must be free to use. And it is just because artists must be free to use violence —a legal right that is beginning to come under attack—that we must also defend the legal rights of those filmmakers who use violence to sell tickets, for it is not the province of the law to decide that one man is an artist and another man a no-talent.

PAULINE KAEL
The New Yorker

Why Do They Go to the Movies?

Why does today's young generation go to the movies? Partly for the same reasons any generation turns to fiction. Most people who read fiction do so because they enjoy it. And people like it because it is an image of life and, in the words of Robert Penn Warren, "stimulates and gratifies our interest in life." People also like fiction because they are always interested in a good fast story.

Fiction as dream: a critique

> Even when we read, as we say, to "escape," we seek to escape not from life but to life, to a life more satisfying than our own drab version. Fiction gives us an image of life—sometimes of a life we actually have and like to dwell on, but more often, and poignantly, of one we have had but do not have now, or one that we have never had and can never have.
>
> The ardent fisherman, when his rheumatism keeps him housebound, reads stories from *Field and Stream*. The baseball fan reads *You Know Me, Al,* by Ring Lardner. The little co-ed, worrying about her snub nose and her low mark in Sociology 2,

dreams of being a debutante out of F. Scott Fitzgerald, and the thin-chested freshman, still troubled by acne, dreams of being a granite-jawed Neanderthal out of Mickey Spillane. When the Parthians in 53 B.C. beat Crassus, they found in the baggage of Roman officers some very juicy items called *Milesian Tales,* by a certain Aristides of Miletus; and I have a friend who, in A.D. 1944, supplemented his income as a GI by reading aloud *Forever Amber,* by a certain Kathleen Winsor, to buddies who found that the struggle over three-syllable words somewhat impaired their dedication to that improbable daydream.

And that is what, for all of us, fiction, in one sense, is—a daydream. It is, in other words, an imaginative enactment. In it we find, in imagination, not only the pleasure of recognizing the world we know and of reliving our past, but also the pleasure of entering worlds we do not know and of experimenting with experiences which we deeply crave but which the limitations of life, the fear of consequences, or the severity of our principles forbid us to. Fiction can give us this pleasure without any painful consequences, for there is no price tag on the magic world of imaginative enactment. But fiction does not give us only what we want; more importantly, it may give us things we hadn't even known we wanted.

ROBERT PENN WARREN
The Saturday Evening Post

Film as dream: a letter

DEAR MR. KUBRICK:

2001 is a story structured like a dream.

The four acts are announced not by raising and lowering of a curtain but by the appearance four times of knowledge, embodied as a Duranodic slab, like the apple tree of Genesis a phallic symbol, the phallus being the instrument of primary creation, as is knowledge that of intellectual creation:

Introduction – the first appearance of knowledge and the first result; the first tool, a weapon, followed by the entire history of man most beautifully pictured as that weapon (tool) rising to the grandeur of a spaceship.

The plot thickens–an overeducated doctor is congratulated on a completely innocuous speech, and he, in turn, congratulates his colleagues on a discovery which took no more initiative than a dog discovering a bone. Knowledge is turned against them. It deafens them. It overwhelms them. So, to discover its origins, they send a ship, captained by a man of humility, calm under pressure, an artist; in short, a hero. Knowledge on board in the form of a computer tries to thwart him. We are not told until the computer is expurgated that it alone knew the purpose of the mission.

Crisis–the hero (*der Held*) arrives at the point of discovery. As we see from the expression on his face, it is a more terrifying experience than his bout with the computer, for, as *we* discover in the final . . .

Resolution–the discovery is not of some strange new world but of himself; the wisdom of age is his rebirth.

But whose dream is it? Yours, of course, but I think you asked yourself if you were so much different from the rest of us and you decided that you were not and so you made a film.

FREDERIC P. LYMAN
Malibu, California

The loss of narrative line

It is not just general audiences out for an evening's entertainment who seem to have lost the narrative sense, or become indifferent to narrative. What I think are processes of structural disintegration are at work in all types of movies, and though it's obvious that many of the old forms were dead and had to be broken through, it's rather easy to see what's happening–and not just at the big picture-palaces . . .

Perhaps now "stories" have become too sane, too explicable, too commonplace for the large audiences who want sensations and regard the explanatory connections as mere "filler"–the kind of stuff you sit through or talk through between jolts.

It's possible that television viewing, with all its breaks and cuts, and the inattention, except for action, and spinning the dial to find some action, is partly responsible for destruction of the narrative sense–that delight in following a story through its complications to its conclusion, which is perhaps a child's first conscious artistic pleasure. The old staples of entertainment–inoffensive genres like the adventure story or the musical or the ghost story or the detective story–are no longer commercially safe for moviemakers, and it may be that audiences don't have much more than a TV span of attention left: they want to be turned on and they spend most of their time turning off . . .

PAULINE KAEL

Generations neatly split

Thought of five years ago *only* as an entertainment form–with a separately delineated category for "art" house imports–movies are now *in* and regarded as a legitimate pursuit in America. In contrast, the more traditional arts such as theater and opera are shaky if not altogether ready to enter an old age home. The lines at the box office are a proof of sorts that film and film alone is attracting kids. Just as it is inconceivable that anyone would stand in line for two hours to see a play or purchase a book, it is taken for granted that one will wait this long to see *Midnight Cowboy* in a city like New York. Legitimate theater, with the exception of such youth-geared musicals as *Hair* and *Salvation,* exerts little if any appeal. And the one-week performance by the Who of their rock-media opera *Tommy* at the Fillmore East is the closest anyone under thirty will get to a tier at the Metropolitan.

To understand the kind of age polarization that has occurred, one has only to glance quickly at the lyrics of two songs: the title number from *Hello, Dolly!* and "Go to the Mirror" from *Tommy*. "It's

From the motion picture *Woodstock* copyright © 1970 by Warner Bros. Pictures, Inc.

A scene from the motion picture *Easy Rider* copyright © 1969. Columbia Pictures Industries, Inc.

so nice to have you back where you belong," sing the waiters in the long-running Broadway musical, articulating a nostalgia and a red-carpeted style of life that seems altogether foreign if not indulgent to the kids who witnessed Woodstock, the Vietnam Moratorium, and the March on Washington. In sharp contrast, the psychologically deaf, dumb, and blind Tommy sings, "See me, feel me, touch me, heal me" from the heavily amplified stage of the Fillmore, and the generations neatly split themselves right down the middle. One has fake cotton-candy dumplings in its mouth, while the other speaks of irresistible pinball wizardry from an electronically vibrant stage.

LARRY COHEN
Saturday Review

Celebrating the Film Generation

So the Film Generation, flaws and all, represents both a circumstance and an opportunity. On the whole it is, I believe, the most cheering circumstance in contemporary American art. That generation can be a vital force, or it can twiddle its strength and chances away in irrelevant artistic nihilism, in engorged social petulance. One does not ask them to "save" film forever. In the long run, the history of the film will be the same as that of all arts: a few peaks, some plateaus, many charms; but the present chance—a rare one—could save much time in the development of this young medium. The foreseeable future is all that, reasonably, we can have hopes or anxieties about in art. The Film Generation can help to make the foreseeable future of film interesting and important. Let us see.

STANLEY KAUFFMAN

Part 2

GETTING ACCUSTOMED TO THE DARK:

What Seems to Be the Matter in the NEW AMERICAN CINEMA

The picture is all personal. Who would do a film
if it wasn't personal emotions and experiences?
To hell with ideas and words. No one listens, anyway.
The only thing people care about today is what they feel . . .
John Cassavetes

*M*A*S*H*. Courtesy of Twentieth Century-Fox Film Corporation.

The concerns of today's filmmakers reflect the concerns of today's young people.

The American involvement in Southeast Asia has spawned and spurred the Peace Movement and made young people very much aware of the violence that is said to be "as American as apple pie." *Bonnie and Clyde, M*A*S*H, Easy Rider, Joe* and other films attempt in very distinctive ways to get to the bottom of violence.

Youth is traditionally idealistic and young Americans are no exception. Even in the midst of depression, war, or affluence, they look forward to a better world. *2001: A Space Odyssey* probing new possibilities for man's expanding consciousness is as much concerned with inner space as outer. *Alice's Restaurant* portrays the search for community and the problems of the surrogate family. And *Woodstock* is a celebration of the incandescent instantaneous community; *Gimme Shelter* is the sobering reappraisal of such a community.

During a period of high national purpose such as a war, an outsider usually is treated with scorn. But today so many young people feel alienated from their own country–for the very highest of motives–that the outsider is often treated with compassion.

Authors and filmmakers have traditionally been kind to the independent minded. Twain, Steinbeck, Hemingway among authors as well as films such as *Underworld, The Informer, The Loneliness of the Long Distance Runner* have treated these people with understanding and compassion. Today in film and fiction the loser–the outsider–seems to be the rule rather than the exception. *Easy Rider, Midnight Cowboy, The Graduate,* and *Five Easy Pieces* present sensitive portraits of outsiders that millions of young people identify with.

Current American directors have learned much from foreign directors such as Fellini, Bergman, Truffaut, Lelouch, Godard, and Kurosawa, whose works attained popularity in America in the late fifties and the sixties. Today American directors have broken away from the stifling studio system by starting their own production companies, and are sometimes making films of great richness and sensitivity. The quality is being recognized: *M*A*S*H,* for example, won the top award at the Cannes Film Festival in 1970.

Film and Violence

Violence in America is a raw fact. Sometimes it is triggered by racial unrest: Watts, Newark, Detroit.

The 1970 killings at Kent State grew out of political dissent. The Weathermen, construction workers, and other extremist groups have added much fuel to an already spreading fire. The Kerner Report, the Walker Report, and other studies have documented and dissected the American penchant for solving subtle problems by "physically vigorous action."

Events have made us conscious of violence as the basis of our entertainments. Not just conflict but violence. Conflict is at the basis of storytelling because it is at the center of life.

From the motion picture *Chisum* copyright © 1970 by Warner Bros. Pictures, Inc.

Story and conflict

A story is not merely an image of life, but of life in motion—specifically, the presentation of individual characters moving through their particular experiences to some end that we accept as meaningful. And the experience that is characteristically presented in a story is that of facing a problem, a conflict. To put it bluntly: No conflict, no story.

It is no wonder that conflict should be at the center of fiction, for conflict is at the center of life. But why should we, who have the constant and often painful experience of conflict in life and who yearn for inner peace and harmonious relation with the outer world, turn to fiction, which is the image of conflict? The fact is that our attitude toward conflict is ambivalent. If we do find a totally satisfactory adjustment in life, we tend to sink into the drowse of the accustomed. Only when our surroundings—or we ourselves—become problematic again do we wake up and feel that surge of energy which is life. And life more abundantly lived is what we seek.

ROBERT PENN WARREN
The Saturday Evening Post

Conflict and violence

The problem comes when conflict spills over into violence. Saturday morning kiddie cartoons on TV have been criticized for their conflict and violence. Frontier justice and the gangster hero—all with their smoking guns—have become distinctively American institutions.

Angry parents' groups and certain government officials have long asserted that violence depicted on the screen is a cause of real violence. Others believe that vicarious violence is a safe, imaginative channel to let out aggressive feelings. But nobody really knows. Jack Valenti, president of the Motion Picture Association of America, asserts that no definitive study has ever been made to show the effects of pornography or of violence (the "new pornography") on individuals.

Contemporary films deal with violence in a new and distinctive way. *All Quiet on the Western Front* and *Paths of Glory* in their revelation of the irony of war are the forerunners of *The Looking Glass War, The Spy Who Came In From the Cold,* and *Catch-22. M*A*S*H* laughs at war situations. *Bonnie and Clyde* and *Easy Rider,* rather than present stereotypes of violent persons, show violence as something done to human beings. Ironically, alongside these films, *The Green Berets* reduced the Vietnamese conflict to just another good-guys versus bad-guys encounter.

BUTCH CASSIDY AND THE SUNDANCE KID: robbers of the Old West

Like any successful film, *Bonnie and Clyde* was to have its imitators. One of the most successful of these was *Butch Cassidy and the Sundance Kid*, another film over which critics would clash.

> The tone is set early in the picture as Butch and Sundance go clattering down that lovely, lonely valley. "Y'know, every time I see Hole-in-the-Wall again," Butch exclaims, surveying a scene of magnificent desolation, "it's like seeing it fresh for the very first time . . . and whenever that happens I ask myself the same question: How can I be so damn stupid as to keep coming back here?"
>
> Needless to say, Paul Newman delivers this sort of jab with his customary twinkling urbanity . . .
>
> ROLAND GELATT
> *Saturday Review*

Before a big train robbery

The wry, shy, gentle humor of the film is seen in a romantic scene between Butch and the school teacher Etta (who eventually follows Butch and Sundance to Bolivia):

Cut to: Butch and Etta as they pedal along.

ETTA

And after the Flyer?

BUTCH

Sundance tell you about Bolivia?

(Etta nods)

You think I'm crazy too?

ETTA

(She means this)

Not with what they're finding in the ground down there; and if you happen to be a thief.

Butch Cassidy and the Sundance Kid © 1969 by Campanile Productions and Twentieth Century-Fox Film Corporation. All rights reserved.

BUTCH

You're like me, Etta–

ETTA

(She has heard this before)

–sure, sure, sure; I got vision and the rest of the world wears bifocals.

(Butch laughs, leans forward, kisses her gently on the cheek. She looks at him for a moment. Then–)

Butch? Do you ever wonder if I'd met you first if *we'd* been the ones to get involved?

Cut to: Butch.

BUTCH

We are involved, Etta; don't you know that?

Cut to: Etta. He has said this last straight and for a moment now she is absolutely uncertain of herself. Then–

Cut to: Butch.

BUTCH

I mean, you're riding on my bicycle–in certain Arabian countries that's the same as being married.

Cut to: Etta. She breaks out with a laugh, holds him very tight and–

SUNDANCE'S VOICE *(over)*

Hey––

Cut to: Sundance standing in the doorway to Etta's house.

SUNDANCE

What're you doing?

Cut to: Butch and Sundance and Etta as Butch rides close to the house.

BUTCH

Just stealing your woman.

SUNDANCE

Take her, take her.

BUTCH

You're a romantic bastard; I'll give you that.

ETTA

(Whispering to Butch)

I love that man; do you know why?

BUTCH

No. Why?

ETTA

(Ruefully)

I was sort of hoping you did; I sure as hell don't.

WILLIAM GOLDMAN

Butch Cassidy and the Sundance Kid

Butch Cassidy and the Sundance Kid © 1969 by Campanile Productions and Twentieth Century-Fox Film Corporation. All rights reserved.

Symbols, dying

We find ourselves, in a sense, watching *Bonnie and Clyde* over again, with the same stylized treatment of violence. As the two young men, somehow still innocent, lie dying, good-natured kidding pours from them as generously as blood.

This is not a real Western, screenwriter Goldman is saying, and these are not really killers dying, but symbols. This is just the trouble. Artifice and symbolism are no substitute for commitment and solid characterization. In two hours, we know little more about Butch and Sundance than we did before. Their interior life has never been opened to us. Instead, as they lie dying, they remain, somehow, vague unfinished emblems of romance, youth and individuality, once again beaten by the system.

Newsweek

M*A*S*H: the violence of war

*M*A*S*H* combines a setting of bloody casualties (in this case Korea and the Korean War) with the best of the black humor of war. *M*A*S*H* (meaning Mobile Army Surgical Hospital) was made, with extensive changes, from the novel *MASH* written by an anonymous former army surgeon, "Richard Hooker."

> No one sees the war the way the surgeons do, not even the generals. They see big explosions and buildings collapse. But they don't see what happens to the soldiers; the gashed, crushed, torn, mangled bodies of the young men who lie on the operating tables. Only the surgeons see that.
>
> INGO PREMINGER
> Producer

*M*A*S*H*. Courtesy of Twentieth Century-Fox Film Corporation.

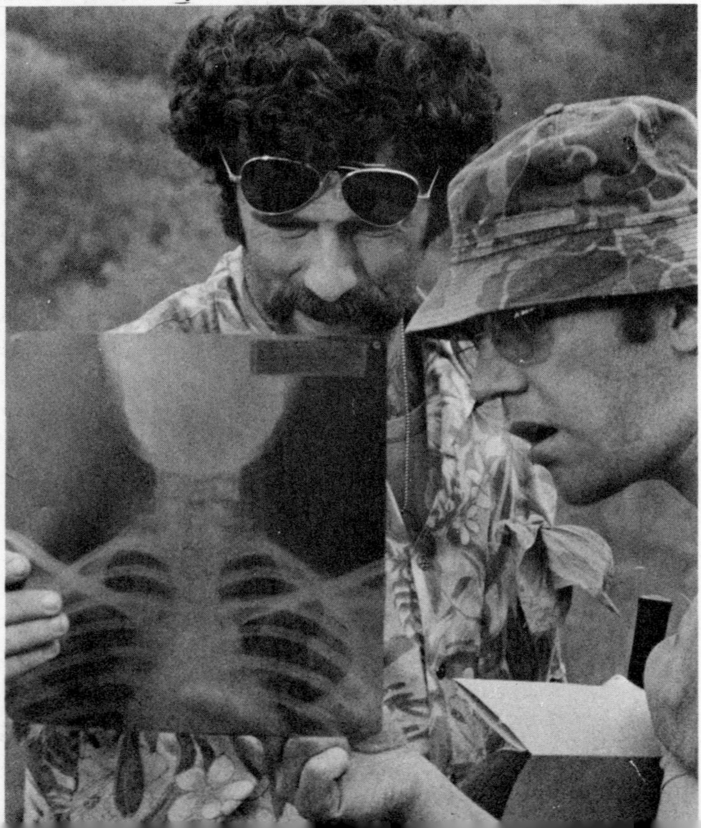

Trapper John, meanwhile, had delved into a chest and Duke was now occupied with several feet of small bowel which were no longer useful to the owner. Hawkeye returned to the preop ward where Colonel Blake had taken charge.

"What's the score now?" Hawkeye asked.

"A major case on every table and ten more that are bad and about thirty that can wait till things quiet down."

"Who's ready?"

"That one over there," said Henry, pointing. . . .

That was the way they played it, day after day. As soon as someone finished a case he had to assist elsewhere until another case of his own was brought in. Then, briefed by Colonel Blake, he'd step in and do his best. When the last of the serious cases was allotted, the surgeons, as they became free, would start working on the minor things—debridement of extremity wounds, some with fractures, some requiring an amputation of a finger, a toe, a foot or a leg, but minor as compared with what had gone before. Meanwhile they, and everyone else, would listen for, and dread, the sound of the six o'clock chopper. . . .

"What the hell is going on up there, anyway?" Colonel Blake asked no one in particular one 6:00 P.M., the roar of the choppers filling the postop ward, where the colonel was assessing results with the Swampmen.

"The Chinks," Trapper John said, "are obviously holding a Gold Star Mothers membership drive."

"And it's up to us," Hawkeye said, "to stamp out that organization, so let's get to it."

"Right," Duke said. "We can fix 'em just as

fast as they can shoot 'em."

"Right, hell," Henry said. "You guys can't go on like this forever. You haven't had any sleep."

"Right," Duke said.

"How the hell do you feel?" Henry said.

"Better than the patients," Duke said.

"Then what the hell are you doing, standing around here?" Henry said . . .

RICHARD HOOKER
MASH

M*A*S*H: anti-war?

*M*A*S*H* begins where other anti-war films end—after the shells have exploded. Only two shots are fired in the movie, and both come from a referee's starting gun during a hilariously corrupt intraservice football game. Instead, there are the results of

*M*A*S*H*. Courtesy of Twentieth Century-Fox Film Corporation.

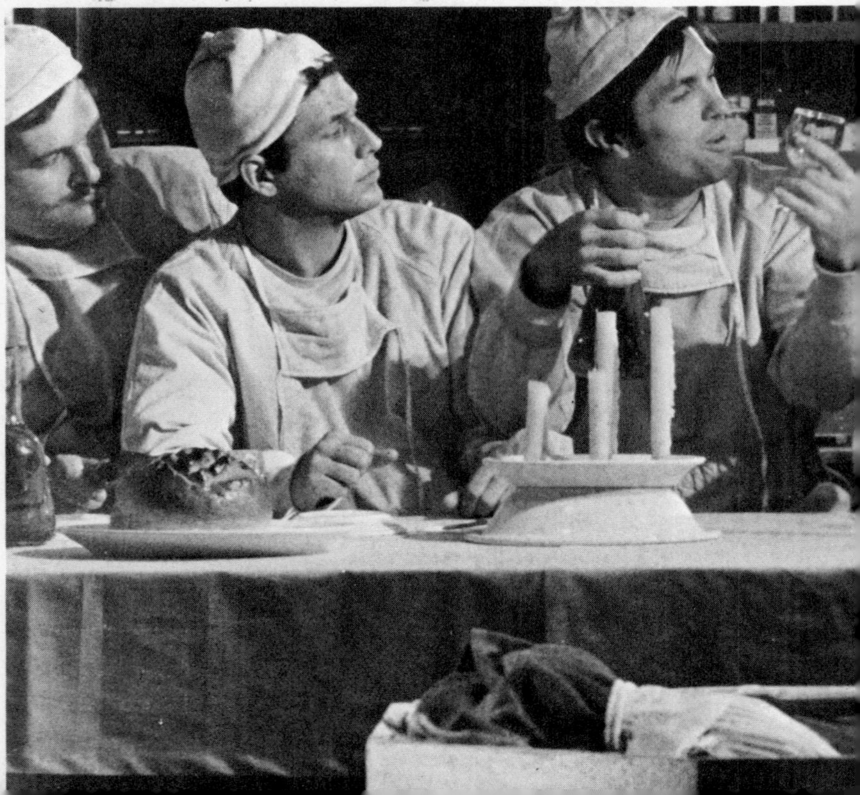

bullets: men bleed on-camera in great arterial gushes. The wounded are flown in on helicopters and stain their sheets as they die silently. The film's two main characters retain their sanity the way men have always done in the shadow of death, with a gallows humoresque.

At the 4077th Mobile Army Surgical Hospital, nothing is sacred because everyone is scared–of the incipient madness that seeps back from the front.

Time

*M*A*S*H* is not the usual anti-war film, since the effects of war–wounded and mangled men–are its environment. Also the humor of *M*A*S*H* is for the most part civilian humor, a bit reminiscent of the medical school antics of a film like *Carry on, Nurse*.

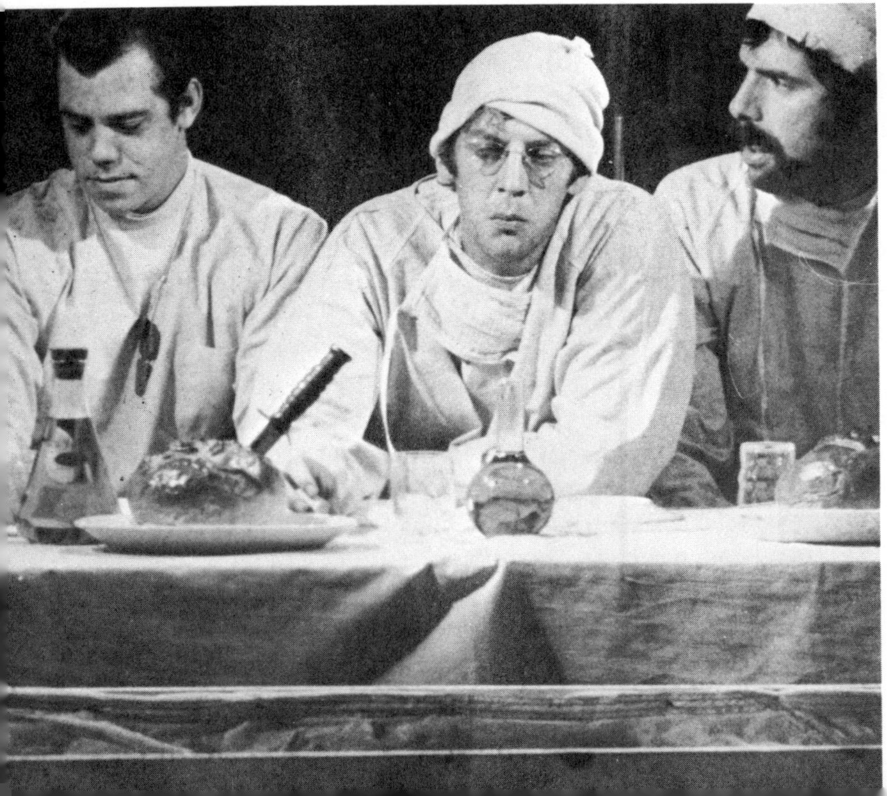

"Robin Hoods of rationalism"

In its infinite, mysterious wisdom, the Army has established a MASH unit in what must be the largest mud puddle of the Korean war. Moreover, it has assigned to it a group of irredeemably civilian medicine men, caught up in the doctors' draft and determined *a*) to practice all the best and latest techniques of their profession and *b*) to retain as much as possible of the freewheeling atmosphere of their medical school dormitories.

But the good guys are not just a bunch of merry pranksters. They are best understood, I think, as Robin Hoods of rationalism, robbing from the rich stockpiles of madness controlled by the people who manage wars and doling it out in lifesaving doses to the little guys caught up in the mess. Vicious in their persecution of the pompous, they have a wonderful tenderness with outcasts and innocents. They manage a miraculous cure for a dentist who is suicidal over an imagined loss of virility, they are marvelously kind to a chaplain who is hopelessly befuddled by the sheer speed and amount of living and dying that goes on in their compound.

RICHARD SCHICKEL
Life

*M*A*S*H*. Courtesy of Twentieth Century-Fox Film Corporation.

"Hip but not hopeless"

I don't know when I've had such a good time at a movie. Many of the best recent American movies leave you feeling that there's nothing to do but get stoned and die, that that's your proper fate as an American. This movie heals a breach in American movies: it's hip but it isn't hopeless. A surgical hospital where the doctors' hands are lost in chests and guts is certainly an unlikely subject for a comedy, but I think *M*A*S*H* is the best American war comedy since sound came in, and the sanest American movie of recent years.

PAULINE KAEL
The New Yorker

A scene from the motion picture *Easy Rider* copyright © 1969. Columbia Pictures Industries, Inc.

EASY RIDER: violent society

America's "silent majority" seems to oscillate between apathy and violence. *Easy Rider,* a film conceived and made as a film and not an adaptation, deals with the violent aspects of an American society that the filmmakers seem to think borders on fascistic repression. Like many American stories it is built around a journey. Its theme is freedom—the impossibility of possessing it in America in 1969—and of knowing what to do with it once it's possessed even in part. "When you read about Mark Twain's Mississippi raftsmen and pilots, or Bret Harte's Western gold miners," wrote George Orwell, "they seem more remote than the cannibals of the Stone Age. The reason is that they are free human beings."

Flight from the system

Easy Rider is, in the smallest, sociological sense, a historic movie. In it, motorcycles are for the first time on screen converted from a malignant to a benign symbol, and the kids who ride them are seen not as vandals or threats to the Establishment but as innocent individualists in desperate unavailing flight from The System.

Sheer romanticism? Of course. But then the endless cycle of cycle-gang pictures to which we have been subjected in recent years is also an exaggeration, a commercialized compound of the worst figments of our most dismal imaginings about what's going on across the generation gap. At the very least, *Easy Rider* is a useful corrective. At its inconsistent best, it is an attempt to restate, in vivid, contemporary terms, certain ageless American preoccupations.

RICHARD SCHICKEL
Life

A new version of the Western

The two men straddle motorcycles instead of horses, and they smoke marijuana instead of tobacco. But the central characters in *Easy Rider* are as remote as the freedom they are seeking. Wyatt (Peter Fonda) is a vague, unshaven pothead who likes to refer to himself as "Captain America." His manic sidekick Billy (Dennis Hopper) has a droopy Stephen Crane mustache and shiny eyes fixed on some wild interior vision. Flush from the profits of dope selling, the cyclists symbolically cast off their wrist watches and head for that persistent American symbol of adventure, The Road.

In the course of this alternately acute and naive odyssey, Wyatt and Billy carom from ranch to hippie commune to jail to the New Orleans Mardi Gras. En route, they pick up a Civil Liberties lawyer named George Hanson. As it emerges in the film, the lawyer's part is only a mug shot of a wry, wistful boozer . . .

His elegies for a vanished life are melancholy without being bathetic; his marijuana-flavored description of a UFO takeover of the U.S. is a perfect comedy, within a flawed tragedy.

With the single exception of Nicholson, *Easy Rider*'s authentic force resides not in its professional but its amateur performances. Filming throughout the Southwest, first-time Director Hopper let the townspeople "rap" as they pleased, then caught them on camera. The result is a harrowing gallery of American primitives, from mindless high-school girls to the redneck truck drivers who case the cyclists' long hair and ad-lib: "Looks like refugees from some gorilla love-in . . . We ought to mate 'em up with . . . black wenches. That's as low as you can git."

Ironically, the film has less to say when the stars step forward. Their visit with the hippies is sticky and overlong . . .

In terms of contemporary mores and methods, *Easy Rider* has told its story from the far side of the generation gap. For once the aura of evil that clings to drug-and-motorcycle movies is gone. Like other films directed to–and by–youth, *Easy Rider* could have settled for catcalls and rebellion. Instead the film has refurbished the classic romantic gospel of the outcast wanderer. Walt Whitman might not have recognized the bikes–but he would have understood the message.

Time

A scene from the motion picture *Easy Rider* copyright © 1969. Columbia Pictures Industries, Inc.

An admission of failure

Easy Rider has been criticized for its sentimental pessimism. But the people, the hostility, and the violence all have the ring of authenticity. The human quality necessary to show the tragedy of violence "like it is" does not come from the two main characters. They admit their failure not only to find America but themselves.

> BILLY: Yeah, we did it; man, we did it. We did it. Huh. We're rich, man. We're retired in Florida, now, mister. *(Sighs–chuckles.)* Whew.
>
> WYATT: You know, Billy–
>
> *Cut to: mcs–*WYATT.
>
> WYATT: –we blew it.
>
> *Cut to mcs–*BILLY *lying down–he sits up Right.*
>
> BILLY: What? Huh? Wha-wha-wha–– That's what it's all about, man. I mean, like you know–I mean, you go for the big money, man–and then you're free. You dig? *(Laughs.)*
>
> *Cut to: mcs–*WYATT.
>
> WYATT: We blew it.
>
> *Cut to: mcs–*BILLY *frowns.*
>
> *Cut to: mcs–*WYATT*–he turns bg and settles down on bedroll.*
>
> WYATT: Good night, man.

EASY RIDER
Peter Fonda, Dennis Hopper,
Terry Southern

A scene from the motion picture *Easy Rider* copyright © 1969. Columbia Pictures Industries, Inc.

Differences between the deaths

Undeniably, the movie is horribly effective; its own confusions even add a terrifying and inescapable logic. When the lawyer George Hanson (played brilliantly by Jack Nicholson) is killed, the loss is acute. The movie misses him; it came alive when he appeared, and in a curious way it seems to die when he does. Fonda's and Hopper's destruction elicits a strong response by virtue of the brutality of the act rather than by feelings for the individuals. Ours is a purely visceral reaction to murder, a response we even indulge in. But we have no time to think, no time to sort out the differences between the deaths. Despite whatever Hopper claims were his intentions, the film lurches out of control and so does the audience. There is a distinction that demands time to be thought out: namely, that Hanson was worth more alive than dead, and Wyatt and Billy become emotionally more valuable to us precisely *because* they die. It is a distinction few if any of us are able to make while still in the theater.

LARRY COHEN
Saturday Review

A new appreciation of life

Some contemporary movies exploit violence, but the best ones do not. A new appreciation of life (and of its loss) may be the most valuable lesson. Even a commercial (but intelligently made) war film like *Patton* has been modified by this new consciousness of life and death. The film's makers and the leading actor, George C. Scott, tried to present Patton as he really was—without glorification—as a "magnificent anachronism . . . the pure warrior."

Patton. Courtesy of Twentieth Century-Fox Film Corporation.

Insiders and Outsiders

Social change produces outsiders and insiders. Today's radical becomes tomorrow's conservative. The *status quo* undergoes transformation under the pressure of new forces of change.

Movies themselves are the product of rapid technological change. In order to stay alive financially, film artists have to feed on, as well as reflect, the real world in which they find themselves. Sometimes this means glorifying the past; more often it means reflecting the present, capturing the value system of a generation but somehow also going beyond it.

Something in the culture

Social change is a fact. The civil rights movement proved that old forms and old institutions—even those frozen into law—are no longer beyond challenge. Groups are organized and are demanding that the power now residing in organizational hierarchies be returned to the group, the community. "Power to the People," once the cry of furtive underground anarchists, is now heard across the land. The motorcycle epics that came before *Easy Rider* only crystallized something that was in the culture.

A film like *The Reivers* deals with a boy on the borderline between innocence and experience. It affirms

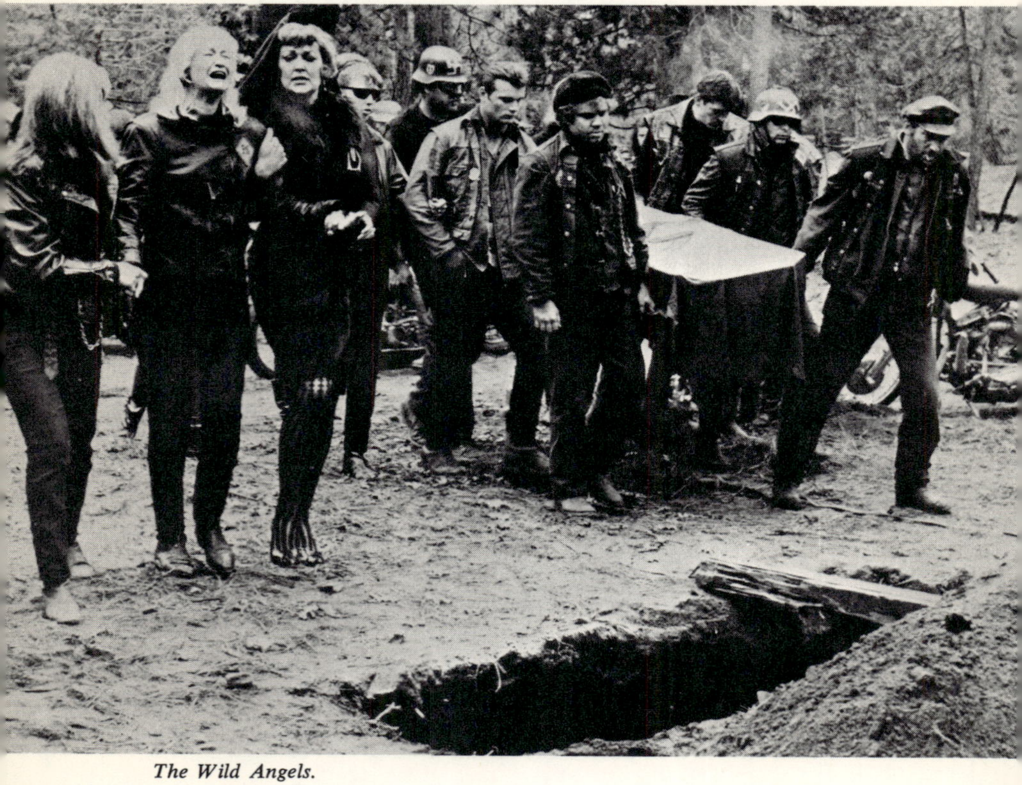

The Wild Angels.

traditional values, such as home and gentlemanliness. Because of its traditional qualities, *The Reivers* has found an audience with the insiders, with Middle America. Lucius, the grandfather, says to the eleven-year-old Lucius McCaslin:

> "A gentleman accepts the responsibility of his actions and bears the burden of their consequences, even when he didn't instigate them himself, didn't say no though he knew he should. Now go wash your face. A gentleman cries too, but he always washes his face."

Ever since Huckleberry Finn, small boys approaching adolescence have been "in" as heroes. But some films, notably Peter Brooks' *Lord of the Flies,* have challenged that assumption. As a nation acquires greater sophistication, its inside and outside groups begin to be treated with meaningful ambiguity—and often as persons rather than as mere cultural types.

Teen-agers in the Andy Hardy movie tradition were insiders as long as they stayed in their place and learned that their parents' values were best for them. The sex-and-sand beach party potboilers represented a change from the Hardy approach, but became as narrowly limited as the world of the Doris Day-Rock Hudson movie. During the past few years young adults have seen the growth of films that mirror and express a new spirit more authentically their own than any before. The Beatles helped with *Help!* and *A Hard Day's Night. The Graduate* became a kind of visual manifesto of the generation gap. With *Woodstock,* a movie celebrated not merely the individual outsider, but an entirely new culture, the outsider community. Through the eyes of its outsider hero, *Five Easy Pieces* brilliantly analyzes the rejection of both decadent "high culture" and the raw but more vital low-down culture of some of middle America.

THE GRADUATE: a homecoming party

"Ben?" he said, opening his son's door.

"I'll be down later," Benjamin said.

"Ben, the guests are all here," his father said. "They're all waiting."

"I said I'll be down later."

Mr. Braddock closed the door behind him. "What is it," he said.

Benjamin shook his head and walked to the window.

"What is it, Ben."

"Nothing."

"Then why don't you come on down and see your guests."

Benjamin didn't answer.

"Ben?"

"Dad," he said, turning around, "I have some things on my mind right now."

"What things."

"Just some things."

"Well can't you tell me what they are?"

"No."

Mr. Braddock continued frowning at his son a few more moments, glanced at his watch, then looked back at Benjamin.

"Ben, these are our friends down there," he said. "My friends. Your mother's friends. You owe them a little courtesy."

"Tell them I have to be alone right now."

"Mr. Robinson's out in the garage looking at your new sports car. Now go on down and give him a ride in it."

Benjamin reached into his pocket for a pair of shiny keys on a small chain. "Here," he said.

"What?"

"Give him the keys. Let him drive it."

"But he wants to see you."

"Dad, I don't want to see him right now," Benjamin said. "I don't want to see the Robinsons, I don't want to see the Pearsons, I don't want to see the . . . the Terhunes."

"Ben, Mr. Robinson and I have been practicing law together in this town for seventeen years. He's the best friend I have."

"I realize that."

"He has a client over in Los Angeles that he's put off seeing so he could be here and welcome you home from college."

"Dad–"

"Do you appreciate that?"

"I'd appreciate it if I could be alone!"

CHARLES WEBB
The Graduate

The Graduate. Courtesy of Embassy Pictures.

Like Wyatt and Billy in *Easy Rider,* Benjamin Braddock was an outsider to middle America but an insider to many young people who shared a different value system than America's over-thirty majority. But *The Graduate* was one of the first films to carry this message. To many traditional insiders the ending of the film was upsetting.

Attack on religion?

In the climactic scene in *The Graduate,* the young anti-Establishment hero bursts into a church where a wedding-of-social-convenience has just taken place, and swinging a large cross to keep the angered relatives and guests at bay, he runs off with the bride —using the cross to bar the door as they make their getaway.

To many, the scene merely adds sacrilege to a film already filled with the sordid, tasteless, immoral adventures of a young man who is not certain what he wants to do with his life.

To others, the scene is a perfect summary of what *The Graduate* is trying to say about modern society's materialistic values and phony Sunday kind of piety. . . .

J. D. NICOLA

A sign of contradiction

For the Christian, the Cross has always meant freedom and strength in defense against the enemy. In this instance, materialistic bourgeois American society is the evident enemy—that monster of hypocrisy culpable for the blasphemy of using the Cross as a symbol of its own spiritless status quo. The peculiar excitement of the scene arises from the gen-

The Graduate. Courtesy of Embassy Pictures.

uine sense of freedom released in Elaine's cry for redemption as she calls on the name of Benjamin.

What Mike Nichols has done here, perhaps unwittingly, is to hold up the Cross as a sign of contradiction which rejects stagnant conformity and hastens the liberation of those who risk everything for the sake of salvation. As a symbol of hope, the Cross becomes the instrument whereby the escapees ride toward a dubious future – an unknown destiny which, nevertheless, is far better than the immobile existence of those locked behind church doors, impotent before the true meaning of the Cross.

REV. JOHN B. GIULIANI
Letter to
The New York Times

Benjamin comes of age

To understand the story it is necessary . . . to understand that Benjamin Braddock belongs to a milieu that has been termed the affluent society. He has never known financial insecurity–he has grown up among gadgets, among cars and swimming pools–and this he has taken so much for granted that it literally has no meaning for him. His parents, on the other hand, had presumably known hard times; they knew the value, for them, of money, of material success, of things. When Benjamin comes of age, literally and symbolically, he finds himself vaguely rejecting all that his parents hold so dear. He finds himself a kind of object, the proud result of proper rearing, a reward of his parents' struggle in his behalf. Somehow, he feels, this is wrong, but he doesn't yet know what is right. What guides and counselors does he have? "Ben, I want to say one word to you, just one word," a friend of the family breathes in his ear at a welcome-home party. Benjamin awaits the word, among clinking glasses holding machine-made ice and good bourbon and scotch. "Plastics," the fellow says, imparting the great secret to success in our time. "There is a great future in plastics. . . ."

He [Benjamin] is a truth-seeker, trying to cut through to some acceptable level of meaning. He even tells the truth to the outraged Mr. Robinson about the affair with Mrs. Robinson: "We got into bed with each other. But it was nothing. It was nothing at all. We might–we might just as well have been shaking hands."

One of the great appeals of the film to the young, and to the young in heart of all ages, is Benjamin's honesty. The most important thing in common between Elaine and Benjamin is that they share the urge to see honestly and clearly.

HOLLIS ALPERT
Saturday Review

With the real people

"Ben?" his mother said. "What are you talking about?"

"I am trying to tell you," Benjamin said. "I'm trying to tell you that I am through with all this."

"All what?"

"All this!" he said, holding his arms out beside him. "I don't know what it is but I'm sick of it. I want something else."

"What do you want?"

"I don't know."

"Well look, Ben."

"Do you know what I want?" Benjamin said, tapping his finger against the table.

"What."

"Simple people. I want simple honest people that can't even read or write their own name. I want to spend the rest of my life with these people."

"Ben."

"Farmers," Benjamin said. "Truck drivers. Ordinary people who don't have big houses. Who don't have swimming pools."

"Ben, you're getting carried away."

"I'm not."

"Ben, you have a romantic idea of this."

"Real people, Dad. If you want the cliché, I am going out to spend the rest of my life with the real people of this world."

"Aren't we real?" Mrs. Braddock said.

"It's trite to talk about it," Benjamin said. "I know how I feel."

CHARLES WEBB
The Graduate

The Graduate. Courtesy of Embassy Pictures.

The symbol of glass in THE GRADUATE

Viewers have made much of the symbolic use of glass and water in the film, signifying Benjamin's inability to get through, to communicate with the generation that has produced him. He peers through the glass of a tank at captive fish. At poolside, and in the pool, he looks out at his parents and their friends through the glass mask of a diving suit. At other times it is through sunglasses that he sees a home environment grown somewhat strange. Surely, Benjamin is alienated, but what is so odd here is that the generation-gappers who love the film regard this sense of estrangement as natural and normal, given the times and the middle-class values espoused by Benjamin's family and friends.

A success with young people

Hollywood has made strenuous attempts to appeal to the young film audience in the past, from Andy Hardy to Elvis Presley. There have been bikini beach parties, rock 'n' roll orgies, Annette Funicello, and Peter Fonda on LSD, but the coin taken in from these usually cheap and sleazy quickies has been but a pittance compared to the returns from *The Graduate*. I need cite only the fact that *The Graduate* has already taken in more than $35,000,000 at the box office, after playing in only 350 of this country's theaters. Marlon Brando, the revered James Dean, and Presley never came near doing that. But this film, without the so-called stars for security, has now done better, financially speaking, than all but a dozen films of the past. . . .

Letters from youthful admirers of the movie have been pouring in on Dustin Hoffman, the talented thirty-year-old actor who plays the unprepossessing twenty-one-year-old Benjamin Braddock. A strong theme of identification with Benjamin's particular parental and societal hang-ups runs through these letters, as it also does in the letters to Mike Nichols, the director with an uncanny knack for forging hits. They've even been writing to Joseph E. Levine, who backed and has been presenting the film. One boy from Dallas wrote Levine, bragging that he had seen *The Graduate* more than any of his friends, no less than fifteen times.

HOLLIS ALPERT
Saturday Review

GOODBYE, COLUMBUS

Another young film, expanded from a Philip Roth novella, was *Goodbye, Columbus*. Resembling *The Graduate* in statement and style, it avoided the romanticized triumphal ending of *The Graduate*. Distinctive about the film was its accurate "translation" of Philip Roth's stiletto-like dialogue, so typical of today's educated young people. As an example of Roth's dialogue we have the hero, Neil Klugman, calling a girl he had only recently met at a country club pool.

A phone conversation

"What's your name?" she said.

"Neil Klugman. I held your glasses at the board, remember?"

She answered me with a question of her own, one, I'm sure, that is an embarrassment to both the homely and the fair. "What do you look like?"

"I'm . . . dark."

"Are you a Negro?"

"No," I said.

"What *do* you look like?"

"May I come see you tonight and show you?"

"That's nice," she laughed. "I'm playing tennis tonight."

"I thought you were driving golf balls."

"I drove them already."

"How about after tennis?"

"I'll be sweaty after," Brenda said.

It was not to warn me to clothespin my nose and run in the opposite direction; it was a fact, it apparently didn't bother Brenda, but she wanted it recorded.

"I don't mind," I said, and hoped by my tone to earn a niche somewhere between the squeamish and the grubby. "Can I pick you up?"

She did not answer a minute; I heard her muttering, "Doris Klugman, Doris Klugman . . ." Then she said, "Yes, Briarpath Hills, eight-fifteen."

"I'll be driving a—" I hung back with the year —"a tan Plymouth. So you'll know me. How will I know you?" I said with a sly, awful laugh.

"I'll be sweating," she said and hung up.

PHILIP ROTH
Goodbye, Columbus

Goodbye Columbus. Courtesy of Paramount Pictures Corporation.

Tell Them Willie Boy Is Here. Courtesy of Universal Pictures.

WILLIE BOY

Tell Them Willie Boy Is Here raises the American Indian from his role as Tonto, or as the victim of a cavalry charge. In the film, Willie Boy, definitely an outsider, is treated with great respect and compassion.

He must die

The central theme is not only clear but runs headlong to its foregone conclusion with the speed and certainty of a falling rock—or more elegantly, with the grim inevitability of Greek tragedy.

Willie Boy, an embittered young Indian whose life has been rendered pointless by the defeat and degradation of his culture, commits an act of violence and is hunted down amid a burgeoning atmosphere of white hysteria. He can neither escape (though his skill makes catching him long and difficult) nor submit to life in a white man's prison. He must die, and he does, nobly. Then the human jackals come and desecrate his grave, searching for souvenirs.

Robert Blake plays Willie Boy beautifully, with all the fatalism and intensity of power-held-in-check that he showed in *In Cold Blood.* Again, he portrays a man hurt, who finally lashes out and must pay the consequences.

JAMES ARNOLD

Ownership and the outsider

The subject is ownership: not of the land, since the Indians never said it was exclusively theirs, but of the people on it. Who owns the Indians? Arthur Kopit posed the same question in his . . . Broadway play, *Indians,* and examined it through an elaborate, allegorical, phantasmagorical version of a Wild West show. Polonsky's scheme is much simpler. Take one Indian, one homely, pool-shooting, match-chomping, girl-lusting Indian who has somehow got it into his head that he owns himself. Trap him between cultures, and eras as well, in a time of transition vaguely analogous to our own—1909, the increasingly popular period of *Butch Cassidy and the Sundance Kid* or *The Wild Bunch.* Then put the screws of paternalism on him, try to keep him in his place, pursue him when he leaves it with an Indian girl, run him down and force him to destroy himself in a hopeless attempt to assert his own existence. "You can't beat them, Willie, never!" cries the girl. "Maybe," he says, "but they'll know I was here. . . ."

Apparently both script and book deal with a true incident, and there's an eerie topicality to this fear of Presidential assassination in a violent America of sixty years ago. But fact must be developed as craftily as fiction. Polonsky never develops the white paranoia that leads to Willie's death. He just drops it in, like a cyanide pellet.

JOSEPH MORGENSTERN
Newsweek

MIDNIGHT COWBOY: friendship between outsiders

Friendship between outsiders, regardless of their external degradation, can be a beautiful thing, even where a close identification cannot be made between the film's characters and the audience. Such an example is John Schlesinger's film masterpiece, *Midnight Cowboy,* adapted from James Leo Herlihy's novel.

In Ratso's place

"Come on, I'll show you already."

They started to walk uptown together. Joe said, "I don't want to stay with you. You think I'm soft in the brain, stay with you?"

Ratso paid no attention to these protests. "It's got no heat," he said, "but by the time cold weather comes, I'll be in Florida. So what do I care, right?"

"I'd have to be out of my goddam mind," Joe said. "You'd sell the teeth right out o' my head while I'ze sleepin'."

"Actually, I don't have no beds, either. But I got enough blankets to smother a horse."

"That how you gonna do it, eh, you crooked little turd? Smother me to death? Just you try it."

"An' I don't bother with no electric. To hell with it, I got candles. Right?"

Bit by bit, Joe began to understand Ratso's living conditions.

In New York there are always a large number of tenement buildings being emptied for eventual demolition. One by one the families are moved out, and as they leave, the owner, a great corporation, has a large white X taped across each window of the evacuated space. Ratso had been living in a series of these X-flats—as he called them—since he'd left home at the age of sixteen.

Midnight Cowboy. Courtesy of United Artists Corporation.

His current dwelling was in a largely Puerto Rican block in the West Twenties. He took Joe there, led him up two flights of stairs to an otherwise vacant floor and down the hall to a little flat in the rear.

The late afternoon sun still gave some light to the room, and Joe found the place more welcoming than anything he'd slept in in weeks. . . .

Ratso was eager to demonstrate the graces of his situation. He offered Joe a chair and then set to work with a saucepan of water and some canned heat to brew up powdered coffee for his guest. Joe headed for the chair but walked right past it and lowered himself onto the bed of blankets. He started mumbling something about how hard it was, but before he got the sentence out he had fallen into a deep dreamless sleep.

Some hours later, he awakened lost. He knew himself to be lying face to the wall in a strange, nearly dark room where a candle flame cast weird shadows on the walls and ceiling. But where? He turned slowly and found himself on a makeshift bed on the floor. Next to him, clad in corduroys, was a pair of poorly matched legs that he began to recognize.

Ratso was sitting there in the candlelight leaning against the wall, smoking, examining Joe's radio.

Joe sat up and snatched the radio from him. He turned it on to make certain it was undamaged. Then he switched it off again and held it close to his body.

"Where's my boots?" he said.

They were under the table. Ratso pointed at

them.

"How'd they get off me?"

"I *took* 'em off ya."

Joe looked at the boots again, and then at Ratso. "What for?"

"So's you could sleep is all. I mean, *cripes!*"

JAMES LEO HERLIHY
Midnight Cowboy

How the film director showed the relationship

Oh, there is a good deal more to *Midnight Cowboy* than a depressing film about raunchy people. It is not the kind of film one can recommend unqualifiedly. It may be the year's finest film, and in the depth that it can move you, an experience no one should miss. But it is a hard film. Schlesinger says a great deal for companionship—the sudden smile that lights the men's faces when they rediscover each other after a long separation, the spontaneous clasp of Rizzo's arm. Rizzo's quiet, spontaneous embrace of Buck when he is scared and in pain. He says a great deal for growing out of fantasy—for this is what Joe eventually does, throwing away his adornments. But there is no shirking the dreadful cost of such maturity—the depravity of oneself, the brutalization of another. And, in the final image, there is no looking away from the fact that even victory, while remaining a victory and a redemption, even an entry into a promised land, is tagged with defeat and alone-ness . . . and somehow, I cannot yet say how but I really believe it is there, a hard, incredible dignity.

The outsider, alone in New York

Ideally, *Midnight Cowboy* ought to be seen after a long visit in New York City—and, as you might guess, that's the way I saw it. Most of the film was shot on location in Manhattan, and its touches and allusions more or less take your location there, or your familiarity, for granted. When Joe Voight, the cowboy, encounters a drunk (or dead?) man lying unnoticed on Fifth Avenue (and in front of Tiffany's yet!) or when Dustin Hoffman pauses in mid-street to demand a cabbie's respect for his right to cross the street, a kind of familiar relationship is established with the audience, beyond the humor and fine acting involved. It's like watching a home movie, and walking out of the film is also walking back into it.

Most of all, *Midnight Cowboy* is a New York picture because it deals with alone-ness. Not just loneliness, for in fact you need not be literally alone to experience it—but a jungle code of self-sufficiency, a very carefully defined isolation from everyone else. It is the life-code of any huge city, but New York's has its unique style. For those tough or wealthy enough, it is a protection and ultimately perhaps a real advantage. For the weak and poor it is a cold flame that either hardens or consumes.

GEORGE WEAD

The friendship grows

For the first time in his life he felt himself released from the necessity of grinning and posturing and yearning for the attention of others. Nowadays he had, in the person of Ratso Rizzo, someone who needed his presence in an urgent, almost frantic way that was a balm to something in him that had long been exposed and enflamed and itching to be soothed. God alone knew how or why, but he had somehow actually stumbled upon a creature who seemed to worship him. Joe Buck had never before known such power and was therefore ill equipped to administer it. All he could do was taste it over and over again like a sugar-starved child on a sudden mountain of candy: cuss and frown and complain and bitch, and watch Ratso take it. For that's the way in which power is usually tasted, in the abuse of it. It was delicious and sickening and he couldn't stop himself. The only thing the runt seemed to demand was the privilege of occupying whatever space he could find in the tall cowboy's shadow. And casting such a shadow had become Joe Buck's special pleasure . . .

JAMES LEO HERLIHY
Midnight Cowboy

From the motion picture *Woodstock* copyright © 1970 by Warner Bros. Pictures, Inc.

WOODSTOCK: a nation of outsiders

But what happens when the outsiders – who today seem to be the majority of youth and their over-thirty sympathizers–organize themselves into another inside group? Maybe Woodstock and the national demonstrations and marches can provide a clue.

The beginning of a new nation

The baffling history of mankind is full of obvious turning points and significant events: battles won, treaties signed, rulers elected or deposed, and now, seemingly, planets conquered. Equally important are the great ground swells of popular movements that affect the minds and values of a generation or more, not all of which can be neatly tied to a time and place. Looking back upon the America of the

’60’s, future historians may well search for the meaning of one such movement. It drew the public’s notice on the days and nights of August 15 through 17, 1969, on the 600-acre farm of Max Yasgur in Bethel, N.Y.

What took place at Bethel, ostensibly, was the Woodstock Music and Art Fair, which was billed by its youthful Manhattan promoters as “An Aquarian Exposition” of music and peace. It was that and more—much more. The festival turned out to be history’s largest happening. As the moment when the special culture of U.S. youth of the ’60’s openly displayed its strength, appeal and power, it may well rank as one of the significant political and sociological events of the age.

Time

From the motion picture *Woodstock* copyright © 1970 by Warner Bros. Pictures, Inc.

From the motion picture *Woodstock* copyright © 1970 by Warner Bros. Pictures, Inc.

Woodstock was not a single isolated event. Youth communes celebrated and criticized in *Easy Rider* and *Alice's Restaurant* revealed a developing crisis of community. At Woodstock a community happened spontaneously, but it was a community incomprehensible to many adults.

The consequences of Woodstock

To many adults, the festival was a squalid freakout, a monstrous Dionysian revel, where a mob of crazies gathered to drop acid and groove to hours of amplified cacophony. In a classic example of its good gray mannerisms, The New York *Times* in an editorial compared the Bethel pilgrimage to a march of lemmings toward the sea and rhetorically asked: "What kind of culture is it that can produce so colossal a mess?" But even the *Times* can change its tune. Next day, it ran a more sympathetic editorial that spoke kindly of the festival as "essentially a phenomenon of innocence."

There were, of course, certain things to deplore about Bethel. Three people died—one from an overdose of drugs, and hundreds of youths were freaked out on bad trips caused by low-grade LSD, which was being openly peddled at $6 per capsule. On the other hand, there were no rapes, no assaults, no robberies and, as far as anyone can recall, not one single fight, which is more than can be said for most sporting events held in New York City.

The real significance of Woodstock can hardly be overestimated. Despite the piles of litter and garbage, the hopelessly inadequate sanitation, the lack of food, and the two nights of rain that turned Yasgur's farm into a sea of mud, the young people found it all "beautiful." One long-haired teen-ager summed up the significance of Woodstock quite simply: "People," he said, "are finally getting together." The undeniable fact that "people"—meaning in this case the youth of America—got together has consequences that go well beyond the festival itself.

Time

A special community

More important, Bethel demonstrated the unique sense of community that seems to exist among the young, their mystical feeling for themselves as a special group, an "us" in contrast to a "them." The festival was widely advertised, but the unexpectedly large crowd it attracted suggests that the potential significance of the event was spread by a kind of underground network. "If you were part of this culture," said one pilgrim back from Bethel, "you had to be there." In spite of the grownup suspicions and fears about the event, Bethel produced a feeling of friendship, camaraderie and—an overused phrase—a sense of love among those present. This yearning for togetherness was demonstrated in countless major and minor ways: the agape-like sharing of food and shelter by total strangers; the lack of overt hostility despite conditions that were ripe for panic and chaos; the altruistic ministrations of the Hog Farm, a New Mexico hippie commune which took care of kids on bad trips. If Bethel was youth on a holiday, it was also a demonstration to the adult world that young people could create a kind of peace in a situation where none should have existed, and that they followed a mysterious inner code of law and order infinitely different from the kind envisioned by Chicago's Mayor Daley. In the end, even the police were impressed. Said Sullivan County Sheriff Louis Ratner: "This was the nicest bunch of kids I've ever dealt with."

Time

Making a film about Woodstock

Filmmakers were on the scene at Woodstock, and the resultant footage was edited into a colossal three-hour testament to the event itself. The filmmaker this time was a young man, Michael Wadleigh, subsidized by Warner Brothers/Seven Arts.

Making a film about a primarily theatrical event presents many problems. Movies must move; the stage speaks or sings. Few plays "translate" well to film. *Woodstock* was built around a staged event but was not itself staged. *Woodstock* tried to capture the spirit of the happening; some who were there thought it did; others did not. Critics, some wearing earplugs, were split on the merits of the film as a film. Most liked it.

A documentary film

Woodstock is far more than a sound-and-light souvenir of a long weekend concert. Purely as a piece of cinema, it is one of the finest documentaries ever made in the U.S.

Making the movie was an enormous and sometimes haphazard undertaking. Director-Cinematographer Michael Wadleigh organized a 25-man crew on only a few days' notice, shot over 120 hours of footage, then edited it all down in a frantic seven months. It is no small tribute to Wadleigh's dexterity that the film's three-hour running time passes with the mesmerizing speed of a Jimi Hendrix guitar solo . . .

Wadleigh is equally successful at conveying the sociological aspects of the event through concise interviews with townspeople, festival organizers, police and members of the audience. Everyone from a chief of police to a maintenance man for the Port-O-San portable toilet corporation gets his say. *Woodstock*, however, is not an unrelieved celebration. For every shot of easy affection in the grass and innocent group bathing in the nude, there is a scene in the medical tent, or the ominous voice of the onstage announcers: "The word is that some of the brown acid being passed around is very bad stuff . . . Will Helen Savage please call her father at the Glory Motel in Woodridge?"

Time

From the motion picture *Woodstock* copyright © 1970 by Warner Bros. Pictures, Inc.

The new in-group

Certainly one doesn't get the feeling of jam-packed music talent exploding on stage without end: the over-all note is of self-congratulation, a kind of aren't-we-beautiful running commentary without a clue to what made things so special. What should have been revelation, alas, bogs down, through sheer attenuation, into smuggery.

JUDITH CRIST
New York Magazine

A festival in film

Could a strip of film three hours and four minutes long ever hope to recapture last summer's trip-out at Bethel? It could and it did. I came away from it feeling, quite simply, free.

It is the most sensual, visceral film I have ever seen.

Woodstock has the effect of scooping up your psyche, your hangups, your frustrations and shattering them against the screen. From the opening sequence to the last strains, a boundless energy lopes out at the viewer, diffused through 16-mm. film blown up. The color is glorious, the photography no less than superb . . .

But best of all is the music, enhanced through Wadleigh's camera techniques and excellent editing. The sound is probably far better than anyone could have heard at the festival itself, which might tend to make the film superior to it in that respect. The double, triple and superimposed images, rather than detracting from the musical performances, focus on individual movements, solitary facets, fingering, facial expressions, and in so doing pull the viewer smack into the music. If anything is wrong with the musical segments, it is that footage has not been included from such groups as Blood, Sweat and Tears, the Grateful Dead, and from Jefferson Airplane's incredible two-and-a-half-hour session.

Three performances stand out. Country Joe, who comes out on the platform tall, regal, super-cool, so together that the others pale by comparison. Country Joe with his "Fixin' To Die Rag," still the very best Vietnam parody around. Then there is Mike Shrieve, 19-year-old drummer for Santana, with upturned nose and freckles. There is nothing teenybopper about what he pulls from those drums, and his face is sheer ecstatic delight. At one point the screen splits, and Shrieve's performance is registered as a symmetrical mirrored effect–silver, slick and hard as anthracite.

And, finally, there is Crosby, Stills, Nash and Young, whose "Suite: Judy Blue Eyes" is slightly off-key, musically not as perfect as the record, but so incredibly sad and sensual. "Judy Blue Eyes" is as good as anything Bach ever wrote.

MARNI BUTTERFIELD
Show

ALICE'S RESTAURANT: it started with a song

Arlo Guthrie, at 22 and without even trying, became a new folk hero. His first claim to fame, besides being Woody Guthrie's son, is a song he wrote in 1966.

> Now it all started two Thanksgivings ago . . . when my friend and I went up to visit Alice at the restaurant. But Alice doesn't live in the restaurant, she lives in the church near by the restaurant, in the bell tower with her husband Ray and Facha the dog.
>
> And livin' in the bell tower like that . . . and havin' all that room (seein' as how they took out all the pews), they decided that they didn't have to take out their garbage for a long time.
>
> We got up there and found all the garbage in there and we decided that it'd be a friendly gesture for us to take the garbage down to the city dump . . . well, we got there and there was a big sign and a chain across the dump sayin' "This dump is closed on Thanksgiving." And we'd never heard of a dump closed on Thanksgiving before, and with tears in our eyes we drove off into the sunset lookin' for another place to put the garbage.
>
> Arlo Guthrie's "Alice's Restaurant"

In his droll, fanciful "talking blues," Arlo Guthrie goes on to recount how he was arrested for littering, locked in the Stockbridge, Mass., jail and convicted by a blind judge ("a typical case of American blind justice"), and how this conviction eventually disqualified him for the draft. In the song's mixture of whimsy and anger, moral outrage and absurdist humor, thousands of disaffected and disillusioned young people recognized themselves and their own responses to American life.

PAUL ZIMMERMAN
Newsweek

Alice's Restaurant. Courtesy of United Artists Corporation.

The whole scene

Guthrie might have disappeared from view—another discarded hero—had not a perceptive director, Arthur Penn *(Bonnie and Clyde),* decided to make a movie about the whole commune scene, revolving around the real Alice's restaurant and a recently deconsecrated Episcopal church.

Alice and Ray Brock, former teachers at the progressive Stockbridge School, had become surrogate parents to a community of intelligent, confused middle-class kids—the same kids who would troop to the Woodstock Music Festival by the hundreds of thousands, America's wandering army of the young—unimpressed by affluence, opposed totally to the war in Vietnam, horrified by the prospect of middle-class life and desperate to find an alternative.

PAUL ZIMMERMAN
Newsweek

Most people in *Alice* play themselves

Arlo Guthrie is not the greatest singer of his generation—"I sing as bad as Woody" is the way he puts it—and he is not the finest songwriter of his generation. And, far from being the finest actor of his generation, he cannot really act at all. But, with his muted wit and his eloquently understated rage, his freewheeling life style, he is not so much a spokesman or leader as an embodiment of what has almost instantly been labeled the Woodstock generation.

"Arlo has the same problems and he's going through the same things we are," says 20-year-old Ron Kowalke of Chicago, waiting to see *Alice's Restaurant* for the second time. "Like he goes to this school where people rap on his hair. He wants to get his thing together and find out where he's going." In New York, 17-year-old Danny Weiss, dressed in the youth uniform of denim pants and jacket, put it this way: "Things in this country have gotten to the point where it's such a farce that it has to be funny. You either laugh or go crazy and that's what Arlo does—laughs."

Arlo is nobody's stereotype

For Arlo and his friends, good things are either "out-a-sight," "far out" or "groovy"; bad things are invariably "plastic" or "bring downs." And while this argot is used to cover practically every reaction, everyone seems to know what the other person means.

Yet Arlo Guthrie is not strictly representative of his generation. The world pays him for his fantasies—about his trip off the edge of a cliff on a motorcycle ("I don't want to die/I just want to ride my motorcy—cle"), or his surrealistic visit to the Whitehall induction center in New York—and Arlo lives these fantasies. Recently he returned to his guest house with two sacks containing $500 in rolls of quarters. Arlo was going to pay the deposit demanded from a phone company fearful of young men with long hair by presenting a barrel full of change, naïve in his certainty that the phone company would have to accept mountains of loose silver . . .

PAUL ZIMMERMAN
Newsweek

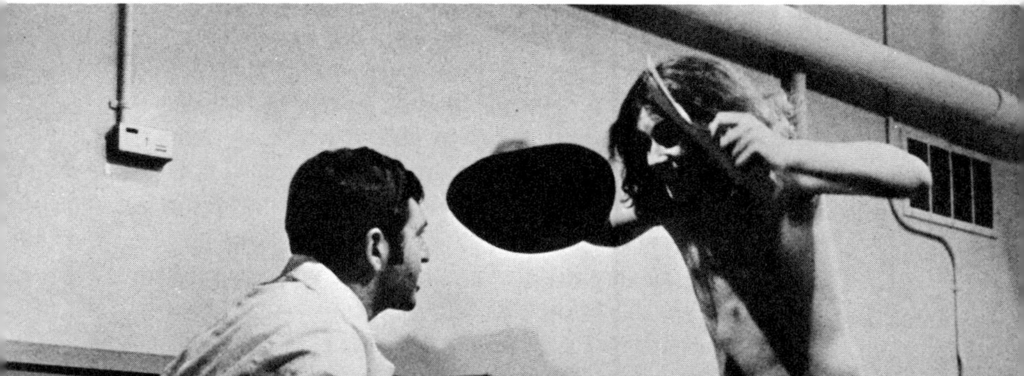

Alice's Restaurant. Courtesy of United Artists Corporation.

Alice's Restaurant. Courtesy of United Artists Corporation.

A new breed of Americans

In the final analysis . . . *Alice's Restaurant* is not about Obie or even Alice and Ray, but about a new, searching, restless breed of young Americans—and it is the most perceptive, balanced picture of this world we have to date. Penn's movie does not paint the Stockbridge experiment in falsely glowing colors. Many of the kids are merely lost souls, clinging to the strength of Alice and Ray, and the whole film is shrouded in an atmosphere of melancholy isolation. "It's a very sad movie," says James Broderick. "I love the kids but I feel very sad about them. They have their life up there. It's what they want. There's a lot of peace, but somehow it's sad." Adds Penn: "If this film says anything, it's meant to show these kids as both hung up and free."

Penn does not see them as a lost generation. "They're not simply dropping out," he says of the Stockbridge kids who have taken jobs as carpenters, artisans, construction workers. "They're using their anger at the world—their disillusionment—in a very constructive way. Their response to Vietnam and the ugliness around them has been to say, 'OK, let's make something beautiful.' This kind of life style isn't viable beyond a stage, perhaps, and it's dependent on the affluence around them. But these kids belong to America. They belong no place else. It's an indictment of America that these kids can't follow their own sense of honesty and still live in our society. We've heard all their indictments before—every generation makes them—but what's original about them is the way they live as a response to our society."

The end of the film does not give an "answer" but asks a question.

Unanswered questions

Alice's Restaurant ends with the world in pieces. Arlo leaves, heading in no particular direction. Alice stands alone before the church—neither young nor old. Ray's dream of utopia is shattered. American culture and the youth counterculture hang suspended in precarious balance. Perhaps, with the affluence that comes from his music, Arlo will be able to realize his pastoral dream of independence in a green place, an American dream rooted in Thoreau, Emerson and Whitman. Perhaps the young man with the cloud of a terminal disease over his head will escape both fate and society. But what about the other kids who sooner or later will have to capitulate to the demands of economics, and what about the Alices and Rays, the young men and women in their late 20's and early 30's who are searching, too, for a new life? And what about America in 1969, split between Arlo's generation and a straight world fearful of its own sons and defensive about its own values? *Alice's Restaurant* and Arlo Guthrie ask these questions that the rest of us must inevitably answer.

PAUL ZIMMERMAN
Newsweek

Old and New Heroes

Every generation must have its heroes, those people who in their life and personality embody and reflect the values, yearnings, and frustrations of virtually everyone else. Yesterday's heroes seemed to stick around a little longer. They became deified and finally crystallized into popular myth. Today's generation, caught up in a time of change whose speed is unprecedented in human history, uses and discards heroes like automobiles or razor blades.

The kinds of heroes

For decades the film hero had been the taciturn, lonely, tall-in-the-saddle Western hero, often with one name. He seemed to embody the best, as well as the most deeply felt, values for Americans. But today, youth's insatiable appetite for prototypes has brought to the screen a number of new kinds of heroes.

In 1955 Shane rode off into the sunset, apparently never to return again. Into his place rode a new Western anti-hero, Hud, complete with long-horn Cadillac, bourbon, and women. But now even Hud is gone, gunned down by hordes of uncommitted desperadoes from the "spaghetti Westerns", and even as these disappear in the east—to Italy—other prototypes appear. Loser-heroes, cool heroes, heroes with part of their social equipment missing, and heroes who "hang loose" provide a mythical framework against which the young audience can see and measure itself. Here are some examples of recent heroes.

***SHANE:* the last of the traditional heroes**

The plot of *Shane* is a typical "empire" plot: a rich cattle baron wants the whole valley for himself. This means that the settlers, the despised "dirt farmers," must move out of his way. When the baron finds it impossible to reason with the settlers he hires a deadly skull-faced gunfighter (played by Jack Palance). But Shane comes on the scene as a Galahad, the man with a past but with a rigid code of honor; he fights for justice—putting his life on the line for traditional family virtues. When he rides off into the West with Brandon de Wilde's young voice calling "Shane, come back," innocent America rides with him.

Shane. Courtesy of Paramount Pictures Corporation.

HUD: the "don't-give-a-damn" hero

The producers of *Hud* advertised this film: "Paul Newman *is* Hud." Sometimes the star gets mixed up with the fictional hero and the two become indistinguishable.

Hud. Courtesy of Paramount Pictures Corporation.

The fictional hero and the real actor

> For there are certain actors who have such extraordinary audience rapport that the audience does not believe in their villainy except to relish it, as Brando; and there are others, like Newman, who in addition to this rapport, project such a traditional heroic frankness and sweetness that the audience dotes on them, seeks to protect them from harm or pain. Casting Newman as a mean materialist is like writing a manifesto against the banking system while juggling your investments so you can break the bank.
>
> PAULINE KAEL

Audiences responded not to the pious cant of Hud's old father, Homer, but to a more vital element: the hero as a nihilistic materialistic capitalist who "wants it all" and who has absolutely no social conscience. Hud's last shouted remark to his youthful brother is "The world's so full of crap a man's going to get into it sooner or later, whether he's careful or not." That is Hud's truth. His final action – going into the kitchen, popping open a can of beer, gesturing scornfully toward the audience and slamming the screen door in its face–were seen as heroic by the young audiences of the fifties.

JAMES BOND: the autonomous man as hero

As one of Her Majesty's most faithful secret agents, James Bond was capable and dependable in any situation and under any kind of pressure. Resolute and reflective, cunning and calculating, Bond could be a lady's man or a man's man, a sybarite or a stoic, a karate killer or a torrid lover. He was ready at one moment to play the connoisseur of wines, and at the next to undergo pain and torture to the limits of human endurance. Bond could accomplish anything—"It was part of his profession to kill people"—and was ready to go anywhere duty or adventure might call. The autonomous man may be admired, resented, feared, or loved, but he is never known. James Bond revealed himself to no one. Ultimately, he remained alone, unattached, invulnerable, self-possessed.

Part of his profession

Bond had forgotten his drink. He picked it up and, tilting his head back, swallowed the bourbon to

From Russia with Love. Courtesy of United Artists Corporation.

the last drop. The ice tinkled cheerfully against his teeth. That was it. That was an idea. He would spend the night in Miami and get drunk, stinking drunk, so that he would have to be carried to bed by whatever tart he had picked up. He hadn't been drunk for years. It was high time. This extra night, thrown at him out of the blue, was a spare night, a gone night. He would put it to good purpose. It was time he let himself go. He was too tense, too introspective. What the hell was he doing, glooming about this Mexican, this capungo who had been sent to kill him? It had been kill or get killed. Anyway, people were killing other people all the time, all over the world . . .

Bond's lips turned down. Cut it out. Stop being so damned morbid. All this is just reaction from a dirty assignment. You're stale, tired of having to be tough. You want a change. You've seen too much death. You want a slice of life—easy, soft, high.

IAN FLEMING
Goldfinger

David McCallum as *The Man from U.N.C.L.E.*

ILLYA KURYAKIN: a teen-ager from U.N.C.L.E.

Illya is a highly idealized and exaggerated personality, but his aloneness in the world seems to symbolize for the teen-ager his own position. The world of the spy is a solitary one, and the teen-ager can identify with that world. He sees himself as a figure traveling alone down an apparently deserted road leading to complex and confusing adulthood. A hostile world full of tension stretches out endlessly around him. He finds no lasting comfort and no real friend upon whom he can depend. He exists with his doubts and fears alone.

Illya is detached, mysterious and free. He is not married. He travels the world over and he leads a dangerous but exciting life . . .

Independent and unavailable

Although he is the member of a team, Illya never sacrifices his independence. He fits within the framework of U.N.C.L.E., but he manages to dress and act in an unorthodox way without diminishing the respect of the more typical agents with whom he works.

For many of his admirers, Illya's sex appeal is the major part of his allure. The casual, cool approach, the blond hair, the turtleneck sweater and other informal attire, the provocative smile, the agile movements, the strength and will power in stress, the gentleness and sensitivity at other times are all important ingredients . . .

The fact that he is unavailable adds to his charm. Solo, like an older brother, gets all the girls, but everyone knows it is Illya they really want. He is his own man, belonging to no one and dominated by nothing. He kissed a girl in one episode but only because she insisted and he did not want to be rude. Most of the time he avoids any physical contact with girls and manages to disappear before they bestow their affection as a reward for valor. He is the man with a cold exterior and a warm heart. Brave, fair and loyal, he fights injustice wherever and whenever he finds it.

Why Illya?

"One of the great modern myths is that women yearn for the big, strong, handsome man. Young girls more often get hysterical over men on the weedy side."

When young girls themselves are asked why they find Illya so appealing, they answer: "He is a doll." "He is so adorable and handsome." "He is so confident. He is cuddly and inviting." "He's sexy, sexy!" "He's the greatest." Teen-age boys, on the other hand, say: "Illya doesn't ever lose his cool." "He knows how to treat girls. He can leave them alone without being considered a fruit." "He is always so smooth." "He can handle himself." "He is so strong, but he doesn't look it." "He is a regular guy."

NED HOOPES

BENJAMIN BRADDOCK: the alienated hero with his social equipment missing

Through humor and guileless guile, Benjamin won out and showed up the fraudulently dishonest Establishment for what it is. He did so without having to sell even a corner of his soul.

Dustin Hoffman "plummeted to stardom" as Benjamin. The reviewer in *Saturday Review* put it this way: "Slightly undersized, totally unsmiling, he stares his way through a series of horrendous, harrowing experiences which lead him from first sex to first real and true love."

The graduate

Like many another new college graduate, Benjamin Braddock is alienated. His only distinction is how much he has to be alienated from: a string of scholarly achievements, rich parents, a Beverly Hills home done in California ghastly with materials that God never dreamed of during that heavy week's work, a new Alfa Romeo convertible, a scuba diving suit, and all of it blighted by a suspicion that his only mission in life is to mope.

Webb wrote the character beautifully to begin with, but it is Dustin Hoffman in his first motion-picture performance who turns Benjamin into an endearing, enduring hero. He never seems sure of what his voice, eyes or hands are doing, or whose orders they are following. He wears the world like a new pair of shoes. He nods his head whenever he doesn't quite know what he means, which is often. He is wrenchingly simple and vividly intelligent, even with his self-doubts, and his bumbling seduction scenes with the wife of his father's law partner, elegantly played by Anne Bancroft, are as funny as anything ever committed to film. "Do you find me undesirable?"

she asks in her coolly predatory way. "Oh, no, Mrs. Robinson," he replies, "I think you're the most attractive of all my parents' friends.

JOSEPH MORGENSTERN
Newsweek

The same general type of hero is found in some of the characterizations done by Elliott Gould—in *Getting Straight, Move,* and other films.

The Graduate. Courtesy of Embassy Pictures.

A scene from the motion picture *Easy Rider* copyright © 1969. Columbia Pictures Industries, Inc.

PETER FONDA **and** ***DENNIS HOPPER*****:** **the persecuted hero**

Film is not about reality, but about people's experience of reality. Young people with long hair, jeans, jackets, and cycles certainly feel persecuted in many ways by a very square and insensitive world. In a journey across America from west to east, Hopper and Fonda become new Western heroes. In the end, after all the persecution, they are destroyed.

Tragic ending

One of the film's ironies is that America can no longer tolerate its traditional hero—its seekers, its independent spirit. It must destroy him. For his part, the hero senses that he has not used his freedom, and in not using it, has lost it, has begun to die. Fonda's simple judgment to Hopper, before the tragic ending: "We blew it."

JAMES ARNOLD

Nightmare experience

Hopper's vision is obsessed with death and prostitution from its very first minute on the screen; it senses persecution all around it, and it invites us to join in with our personal nightmares and experiences, our collective paranoia. It says that this is the way this country is, and, cleverly, it shows us the devastating fire and explosions in advance of their actual, sequential appearance that ends the film.

LARRY COHEN
Saturday Review

The plight of freedom

During a lull at a campsite in their journey, Billy (Dennis Hopper) and Wyatt (Peter Fonda) talk about their plight with George (Jack Nicholson), a young alcoholic ACLU lawyer they have picked up along the way:

GEORGE: (*os*) You know—

Cut to: cs—GEORGE.

GEORGE: —this used to be a helluva good country.

A scene from the motion picture *Easy Rider* copyright © 1969. Columbia Pictures Industries, Inc.

*Cut to: mcs—*BILLY *and* GEORGE*—favors* BILLY.

GEORGE: I can't understand what's wrong with it.

*Cut to: mcs—*GEORGE *and* BILLY*—favors* GEORGE.

BILLY: Huh. Man, everybody got chicken, that's what happened, man. Hey, we can't even get into —like—uh—second-rate hotels—

*Cut to: mcs—*BILLY *and* GEORGE*—favors* BILLY.

BILLY: I mean, a second-rate motel. You dig. They think we're gonna cut their throat or something, man. They're scared, man.

GEORGE: Oh, they're not scared of you. They're scared of what you represent to them.

BILLY: Hey, man. All we represent to them, man, is somebody needs a haircut.

GEORGE: Oh, no.

*Cut to: mcs—*GEORGE *and* BILLY*—favors* GEORGE.

GEORGE: What you represent to them is freedom.

BILLY: What the hell's wrong with freedom, man. That's what it's all about.

GEORGE: Oh, yeah; that's right—that's what it's all about, all right.

*Cut to: ms—*WYATT.

GEORGE: *(os)* But talking about it and being it—that's two different things.

Cut to: mcs—low angle: GEORGE *and* BILLY.

GEORGE: I mean, it's real hard to be free when you are bought and sold in the marketplace. 'Course don't ever tell anybody—

Cut to mcs—low angle: GEORGE *and* BILLY—*favors* GEORGE.

GEORGE: —that they're not free, cause then they're gonna get real busy killin' and maimin' to prove to you that they are. Oh, yeah—they're gonna talk to you, and talk to you, and talk to you about individual freedom—

Cut to: mcs—low angle: BILLY *and* GEORGE—*favors* BILLY.

GEORGE: —but they see a free individual, it's gonna scare 'em.

BILLY: Mmmm, well, that don't make 'em runnin' scared.

Cut to: mcs—low angle: GEORGE *and* BILLY—*favors* GEORGE.

GEORGE: No. It makes 'em dangerous.

Cut to: mcs—low angle: BILLY *and* GEORGE—*favors* BILLY—GEORGE *flaps his arms.*

GEORGE: Nik, nik, nik, nik—

Cut to: ms—high angle: BILLY *and* GEORGE—GEORGE *flapping his arms.*

GEORGE: —nik, nik, nik, nik—— Swamp.

GEORGE *lies down, then leans up on elbows.*

GEORGE *and* BILLY: (*Ad lib snickers.*)

BILLY: *(Mutters.)* You're right, man. Whew. Swamp.

Easy Rider

Permanent and emerging heroes

Film heroes, unlike those from novels, have a double identity—the character they play and the personality that they themselves project. In most cases the personality outlasts the character despite the fact that the old Hollywood star system is in decline.

One of the most durable Western-hero types has been John Wayne. Within the limits of the Western, Wayne has gone through three stages.

> Superficially his films have been as alike as buffalo nickels. Only the date changes; even the Indian looks the same. Yet through the decades there has been a perceptible alteration. The public, riding along in movie houses or taking the TV shortcut, has watched the celluloid Wayne pass through three stages of life. In the '30's, he was the outspoken, hair-trigger-tempered son who would straighten out if he didn't get shot first. By the late '40's, he had graduated to fatherhood: top-kick Marine to a platoon of shavetails or trail boss to a bunch of saddle tramps. In *True Grit* his belt disappears into his abdomen, his opinions are sclerotic and his face is beginning to crack like granite. Audiences now recognize him as a grandfather image, using booze for arterial antifreeze, putting off winter for one more day. They also recognize Wayne as an actor of force and persuasion.
>
> *Time*

One reason Wayne is durable is that, as he proved in *True Grit,* he has perspective on himself.

ROOSTER COGBURN: self-parody

At the edge of a birch grove, four mounted outlaws try to stare down the aging lawman.

"I mean to kill you or see you hanged at Fort Smith . . ." barks Marshal Rooster Cogburn.

"Bold talk for a one-eyed fat man," the bandit leader sneers.

"Fill your hand, you sonuvabitch!" Cogburn answers, clamping his reins in his teeth and letting loose with a two-handed fusillade from his Winchester and long-barreled revolver.

At the end of the battle, four villains—and one horse—lie punctured and defunct upon the ground. "Dammit, Bo," says Cogburn to his mount as he lies pinned beneath it. "First time ya ever gave me reason to curse ya."

Self-parody is the price of style. Hemingway verged on it in his later novels; Presidents Roosevelt and Eisenhower accomplished it in their later speeches. John Wayne charges into it in his latest movie, *True Grit*. Like all consummate stylists, he remains unharmed. Only the enemy is hurt.

The broader the parody, the bigger the self. Wayne has been honing and buffing that self in some 250 pictures—mostly Westerns—for 40 years. He has become the essential American soul that D. H. Lawrence once characterized as "harsh, isolate, stoic and a killer."

Wayne's personal philosophy (his politics aside) is primitive American:

Though it was made in this century, it [*True Grit*] has the terse ring of orders from Davy Crockett: 1) always keep your word; 2) a gentleman never insults anybody intentionally: 3) don't go around looking for trouble. But if you ever get in a fight, make sure you win it.

Time

When Wayne finally rides off into the sunset, one real Shane-like hero will have vanished from the scene.

True Grit. Courtesy of Paramount Pictures Corporation.

Alice's Restaurant. Courtesy of United Artists Corporation.

ARLO GUTHRIE: the hero who "hangs loose"

Arlo Guthrie, in *Alice's Restaurant,* prefigures the joy of the Woodstock Nation. One way to deal with an unsmiling monolith is to smile at it. Guthrie (playing himself) is surrounded by death and alienated by stupidity from the world at large. But somehow he still remains joyful.

The same sense of joy in extremely arduous circumstances occurs in *Woodstock.* Appropriately enough, Arlo Guthrie was one of the better performers at Woodstock.

The message from the Woodstock type of hero seems to be: Hang loose, if you get uptight you get shot, so don't sweat it. Sing, laugh, even do your thing. It remains to be seen whether the Arlo Guthrie hero can survive the pressures of a nation in deep conflict. Perhaps a new hero needs to be born. If so, he will be born.

> "I don't get involved in the world outside, man. I create my own. I stay with my friends. We're in the same boat and we don't believe we should get out of the boat. Too many people have been too concerned about everyone else. It's nice to be your brother's keeper but first you have to learn to keep yourself."
>
> ARLO GUTHRIE

Alice is a youth festival

It is happening all over again. Woodstock, last summer's "three days of love and peace," has been re-created in a joyous, volcanic new film that will make those who missed the festival feel as if they were there. Those who actually were there will see it even more intimately.

Time

Nothing makes him uptight

Alice also has its share of deaths: the passing of Woody Guthrie, of Shelley, of a whole way of life personified by the deconsecrated church. But unlike the brutal murders of *Rider,* both the man and boy die off-screen here. Their deaths are presented as a part of life rather than an end to it. Penn's film is vitally and compassionately interested in life and in a sense of humor as a style for coping, for living in Moratorium America without paranoia. Arlo's songs and manner are those of mild ridicule despite the disasters that shroud the film; the music and the style seem healthy, and they wear well.

LARRY COHEN
Saturday Review

The filmmaker as hero

For many young people, turned on to film, the director rather than the star has become the hero—the focus of interest—and is followed closely by knowledgable critics.

> Some of this youthful insistence on relevancy has been invigorating and valuable in that it reflects an outcry against what is truly dated. It has brought us a vital (if not slightly late) awareness that film is primarily a director's medium. Consequently, kids and adults are becoming familiar with the names and works of Arthur Penn, Stanley Kubrick, Sam Peckinpah, and of course Mike Nichols. It has led to an appreciation of criticism: One spectator at this year's San Francisco Film Festival even asserted that the writings of critic Pauline Kael will survive the films of Sidney Lumet.
>
> If we are lucky, this positive education will not stop with the director but will be extended to include an awareness of the components that define filmmaking: Nicholas Roeg's cool, alienating camerawork for *Petulia* (as well as the cinematography of such men as Lucien Ballard, Conrad Hall, William A. Fraker, Laszlo Kovacs, Pasquale de Santis, and Michael Nebbia); Dede Allen's major contribution as editor in *Rachel, Rachel* and *Bonnie and Clyde;* and Lawrence Marcus's brilliant screenplay of lacerated nerves and casual violence for *Petulia.*
>
> Similarly, we are discovering just how a filmmaker like Peter Yates can straddle two theoretically divided kinds of films—the entertainment and the so-called art movie. Superficially a cops-and-robbers film, *Bullitt* on closer examination yields a more complicated and fascinating set of structural parallels between the policeman and the killer. And his new film, *John and Mary,* transforms the banalities

The Graduate. Courtesy of Embassy Pictures.

of an updated romance by complementing them with incisive visual details. By showing, for example, how Dustin Hoffman cracks his soft-boiled egg and eats it scooped out in the cup while Mia Farrow cracks and eats hers from the shell; by taking an overused device like the freeze-frame and showing how it can still be used humorously and originally, the British director draws attention to simple, illuminating bits of action instead of leaving the viewer to rely on dialogue to get his bearings.

LARRY COHEN
Saturday Review

A different kind of emerging hero

Robert Redford is a different kind of emerging hero. As the sheriff in *Willie Boy* or the skier in *Downhill Racer* he portrays the tough, self-interested hero who "comes there" only because he really wants to. *Downhill Racer,* Redford's own film, takes a hard look at a little-recognized sport and in a larger way looks at all of sport:

> From a distance the skiers seem to have the effortless natural grace of birds in flight. Close up, though, he makes us see they are engaged in a brutal, breath-stealing ordeal, and the contrast gripped me as strongly as anything I have recently seen on the screen. Then there's the other paradox—that this agonizing effort takes place, unlike that of any other sport, with the competitor alone in a sea of silence. Only the wind and the oddly peaceful whoosh of his skis on the snow accompany him.
>
> One thinks of these skiers as professionals, which they are of course, by common, winking consent, even though legally they are amateurs. They are pros in everything except name, meaning that they accept the most rigorous forms of discipline (including self-discipline) because they love the sport with an intensity no amateur can—love it so much they are willing to devote their *entire* lives to the pursuit of excellence in it. That they should, as Jean-Claude Killy and the hero of this film do, expect and receive rewards commensurate with their dedication seems to me only honest and realistic. The cynicism belongs to the gray old men who insist on the pious pretense that sport, conducted at this level, is otherwise strictly nonprofessional—mostly because they wish it were.
>
> David Chappellet, as Robert Redford plays him, is such a driven, driving competitor. He races by their

Downhill Racer. Courtesy of Paramount Pictures Corporation.

rules, but he plays life by his own. The good of the team, the honor of the nation, the pleasures of tradition are nothing to him. He's there because he's good—and potentially great—and that's the end of sporting platitudes. Redford gives us a kid who is tough, innocent, vain—a taker who gives of himself only when he's on the hill racing. But then gives all of himself. In short, he is what all great athletes are—an individualist pushing out against the limits of his sport.

He's not an entirely pleasant fellow, but no one hell-bent on radical self-improvement is. The reward for success in this endeavor in sport is, of course, social improvement as well, and Redford knows that the gentleman athlete is obsolete because rude kids who knew what winning could do for them socially and economically elbowed him aside in their effort to earn what was his by birthright. It is this complex figure, rebellious against his coach (Gene Hackman), vulnerable to a sophisticated girl (Camilla Sparv), that Redford gives us in all his surprising depth. He is the definitive jock, one of the central symbolic figures in the inner life of modern men. The intensity of the challenge he flings out, the coolness with which he tries to cover the desperateness of his need to win are sometimes comic. But what he learns in the end, in the moment of his biggest win, about the fleeting nature of victory and the role luck plays in achieving it is not funny at all.

RICHARD SCHICKEL
Life

The anonymous hero

Another possible hero is the ordinary man caught in the middle of an oppressive bureaucracy but not dominated by it. Such a man is the anonymous—or nearly anonymous—hero in *Z:*

> Converted and unconverted alike will be riveted to their seats by the impact of this finest foreign-language film of the year, a fiercely passionate and coolly detailed story of political assassination and of the death of virtue.
>
> And throughout Jean-Louis Trintignant, as the investigating judge, gives us a triumphantly enigmatic performance as the impartial seeker after fact, the noncommittal interrogator who does not allow his eyes to flicker even behind dark glasses, whose ultimate actions come as an astonishment—and yet an inevitable conclusion.
>
> JUDITH CRIST
> *New York*

> By definition *Z* is a polemic. The film plainly exaggerates the horrors of the present Greek scene. But it is a polemic that was created, not just felt, partly by using dialogue that is more like lyrics than speech. According to traditionalist historians, there is no history, only biography. *Z* reverses the proposition; there are only forces, not men. Accordingly, the leading roles are the sort one would find on a chessboard. In an essentially small part, Montand is again Camus-like, at once involved and lofty. Trintignant, more through skill than script, turns the abstract notion of justice into a driven man who would shatter his career rather than bend the truth.
>
> *Time*

As heroes are needed, they will be created. The hero, precisely because he is a hero, will never die—though his face may change a thousand times.

Part 3

MOVING PICTURES:

HOW TO FIX A FUZZY FOCUS

There should be all kinds of films.
In all of the arts, there must be some erasing
of the hypocrisy rampant in our world . . .
There must be a general recognition
that there is a world
we haven't seen in the movies,
a world closer to the way things are.
People are ready for it.
Haskell Wexler

The cinema is the best evening school
for the education of the world.
Ousmane Sembene

What Now, My Love?

No one fully understands, or has fully explained, movies as a distinct, distinctive, and sometimes distinguished medium. Undergrounders Andy Warhol, Robert Nelson and Bruce Baille along with old-time experimenters like Hans Richter, Luis Bunuel and Salvador Dali have probed what they felt were the outer limits of the film. But Jean-Luc Godard continues to make films as if no one in the world had ever made one before. New American experimenters such as Mike Snow continue to explore the space-time continuum in a way that may never prove popular but which will influence films and filmmakers for decades to come.

The assumptions of the way we perceive (and therefore experience) time and space are culturally derived and sometimes quite personal. The pace of life in India often bores frenetic Americans. Eskimos live in a word of acoustic, not visual space. Pygmies live in a world of reduced space and accelerated time. Movies have yet to explore and present these possibilities.

Each film contributes
to a process of self-education,
making me conscious
of the enormous diversity
of life around us.
I find myself trying,
through my films,
to trace the underlying pattern
that binds this life together.
This is the true stuff of the cinema–
this dizzying contrast
of sight and sound and milieu.

SATYAJIT RAY

The experimental films of Expo 67

People did not protest that the "meaning" of the films was not clear, or that they didn't tell a story. They accepted the films as entertaining, informative experiences, and came by the millions to share in these experiences. It is now possible, for this reason, to experiment in the film medium without too great a fear that there will be no audience for the works which push the film idiom towards new boundaries.

But is the same true for the new areas of subject matter being opened up by the contemporary feature film, whether experimental or conventional? Is the audience which now begins to accept *technical* experimentation ready for a similar venture in the *content* of the new films, especially when that direction leads to areas of moral sensitivity?

ANTHONY P. SCHILLACI

A revolutionary director

On the part of directors—and especially young directors—there is a cry for greater freedom to experiment with both controversial form and subject matter. The Aspen Film Conference, held in Hollywood in 1970, revealed a young black director with a revolutionary spirit, Melvin Van Peebles.

> For Van Peebles, these are utterly revolutionary times, and film is first and foremost a powerful weapon. Instead of accepting the corruptions of society as it is by catering to its unfeeling and sated audiences with bread and circuses, the artist must make statements of radical proportions. He must mold his audience into something better, more humanized, so that it can share his own elevated degree of awareness and understanding. This is the vocation of the artist in the modern world.
>
> First as a writer of the blackest of songs and now as a director, Van Peebles has seized upon the moment to express his deep convictions. No matter how much he succeeds in Hollywood, he must keep fighting for ever more money, control and artistic freedom. "I demand the right to have my work be a thesis, not a consensus," he says.
>
> MICHAEL CALLAHAN
> *America*

The finances of film

> There is another factor: the film industry is fighting for its life. The elephantine limbs are being lopped off. This is radical surgery. The multimillion-dollar movies are running out of time and finances simultaneously. In a field in which people talk about "track records," the big budget supercolossals lumber like dinosaurs and finish out of the money time after time. Studios are stopping pictures with millions already invested. The traditional backbone, the broad, middle-class, middle-aged audience, is dropping out of the theaters, year by year, and taking root before the television set. The still mobile under-thirties are, increasingly, going to the movies. For the studios, the youth market is already the major market. Young directors have come up with low budget films and netted high profits. The mathematics are simple: ten pictures costing $500,000 to $1.5 million or ten costing $2.5- to $10-million with the same chances of breaking even.
>
> LARRY COHEN
> *Saturday Review*

Young directors

Recent financial successes by young directors should open the door to fresh talent. Larry Cohen says:

> Arthur Barron, head of Columbia's film school, argues . . . : "These kids are going to create their own industry, film establishment if you will, and gradually become totally independent. They're going to make their own pictures, their own way, for their own audience." Perhaps, but the majors will, in all probability, buy them up as fast as they succeed.
>
> LARRY COHEN
> *Saturday Review*

Using the real

A Hollywood actor remarked recently: "Look, man, acting isn't the thing any more. It's getting out there with an Arriflex and finding where it's at and what it is." It can be done beautifully, as in *Easy Rider,* a case where two actors did go and film their story much as their two motorcyclist "heroes" would have found it. It might have been an even better film, however, had not the filmmakers, Dennis Hopper and Peter Fonda, thrown all their own sympathy to what their drug-oriented protagonists rather vacantly espouse in their search for "freedom."

Hopper and Fonda made sure to find only what they had set out to look for: Wexler allowed public events to assist in shaping an already predetermined story. In the case of *Alice's Restaurant,* Arthur Penn used reality to assist him in restaging what was already, at least partially, a real story. All three, in addition to their artistic objectives, share what in a sense is a documentary approach. Why not, then, avoid the fictional altogether and merely go in for straight documentary?

Presumably it takes an artist to use the real in such a way that it takes on power and meaning. And the wonder of it is that our film companies are now backing this new and fresh exploration of our social and physical environment. What has made it all possible, of course, is a large, new, predominantly young, film-sophisticated audience, presumably ready and waiting to welcome almost anything that does not have the look of the Hollywood pap of the past.

HOLLIS ALPERT
Saturday Review

Blow-up. Courtesy of Marc Gervais.

Youth-oriented film—good and bad

As a result of the youth craze, we are due for a series of films—some good, some bad—that reflect a Hollywood in transition. [We] will witness the release of a mixed bag of pictures that are genuinely topical as well as those that will be lamentably foolish . . .

HOLLIS ALPERT
Saturday Review

Directors and their films

What I know about film has been learned from comic strips as much as from the cinema—the rules of cutting and editing are the same for the comics as for the cinema.

ALAIN RESNAIS

I'm a typed director. If I made *Cinderella,* the audience would immediately be looking for a body in the coach.

ALFRED HITCHCOCK

I am a director . . . that is all. I know myself well enough to know if I ever lost my passion for films, then I myself would be lost. Film is what I am about.

AKIRA KUROSAWA

Movies have now gone past the phase of prose narrative and are coming nearer and nearer to poetry. I am trying to free my work from certain constrictions—a story with a beginning, a development, an ending. It should be more like a poem, with metre and cadence.

FEDERICO FELLINI

To make films is for me a natural necessity, a need similar to hunger and thirst. For certain people to express themselves implies writing books, climbing mountains, beating children, or dancing the samba. I express myself by making films.

INGMAR BERGMAN

My films are circus shows. . . . After the elephant comes the conjuror; after the conjuror, the bear. I even arrange an interval around about the sixth reel because people may be getting a bit tired. At the seventh reel I take them in hand again and try to end up with the best thing in the show.

FRANÇOIS TRUFFAUT

Some Predictions

Among the best critics in America today—at least by some estimates—is Andrew Sarris of *The Village Voice*. While denying that he is a prophet, Mr. Sarris has made some interesting predictions on young people in film, the noise level, film fragments, the world as film set, reality and illusion, fantasy, sex, movie-carnival films, 3-D, and film as a fine art.

An open outlook

I don't pretend to be a film prophet, particularly when the continuing existence of the world itself has been cast into doubt. However, enough trends have been set into motion within the past few years to give us some idea of what lies ahead. Technologically, the film medium is being stretched and diversified to accommodate all the blinding and deafening pastimes of the Now Generation. Light and noise as ends in themselves will undoubtedly increase the strain on the audience's nervous systems, and there will be ever-fainter outcries against the systematic brutalization of the senses. But in the end, youth will be served even at the expense of sight and hearing.

Of course, there is nothing new about noise-making in and out of the movies. Middle-aged moviegoers who complain about the *varoom* motorcycle genre exemplified most earnestly by *Easy Rider* have conveniently forgotten the noisy police-car chases of the '30's. And if rock in all its variants be considered insensate noise-making, so were jazz, swing, and bop in their time. Hence, films of the future will follow to some extent the same cycles as films of the past. Even the contemporary obsession with youth is not as new or revolutionary as it seems. Many people *act* younger today, but movie stars are much older on the average today than they were in the 20's and '30's. Everybody's favorite adolescent, Dustin Hoffman, would have once been considered too worn and offbeat for anything but character roles, and Ali MacGraw of *Goodbye, Columbus* fame might have seemed too mature for college-girl parts in the days when studio turnover was a more rigorous process than it is today. Therefore, the fact that movie audiences may get younger and younger does not necessarily mean that movie stars will get younger and younger. Quite the contrary. With everyone seeking perpetual youth from the cradle to the grave, it may be harder than ever for genuinely (i.e., biologically) younger people to break into the movie industry. Films of the future may consequently reflect youthful values without youthful participation.

Juliette of the Spirits. Courtesy of Marc Gervais.

What films will be like

Films will probably seem more fragmented in the future to those who can remember the past. The one-minute or even thirty-second TV commercial, the three-minute pop single, the four-panel comic strip concentrate so much manipulative technique into such a short attention span that people may become impatient with the more coherent forms of the ninety-minute to two-hour-plus feature film.

And what about sex, nudity, pornography, and all that sort of thing, be it simulated or hard-core? Will the tides of "filth" continue to rise or begin to recede? Is sexual frankness a cyclical phenomenon or a progressive one? Here I must side with those who believe that we are closer to the beginning of sexual liberation than to the end, and now that our society has pried loose the clammy grip of Puritanism from the Pandora's box of pansexuality, it will be difficult to imagine the box being closed again at any time in the foreseeable future. Once Man, be he Adam or Homo Americanus, has tasted of the forbidden fruit, he can never return to his original state of innocence. There may be vestiges of Puritanism in our society even in the year 3000 A.D. There will always be guilt, revulsion, and self-hatred as long as men's and women's erotic fantasies clash with their existential fears. As long as Death continues to cast its shadow over the libertine's revels, the screen will never reflect the joyful liberation of sexuality without at the same time casting a pall of metaphysical despair. Nonetheless, the insatiability of the audience's clinical curiosity about the hitherto privileged privacy of others will know no bounds. Scandal will know no barriers, immodesty no limits. One can imagine a time when society not only tolerates, but demands the ultimate invasion of privacy in the

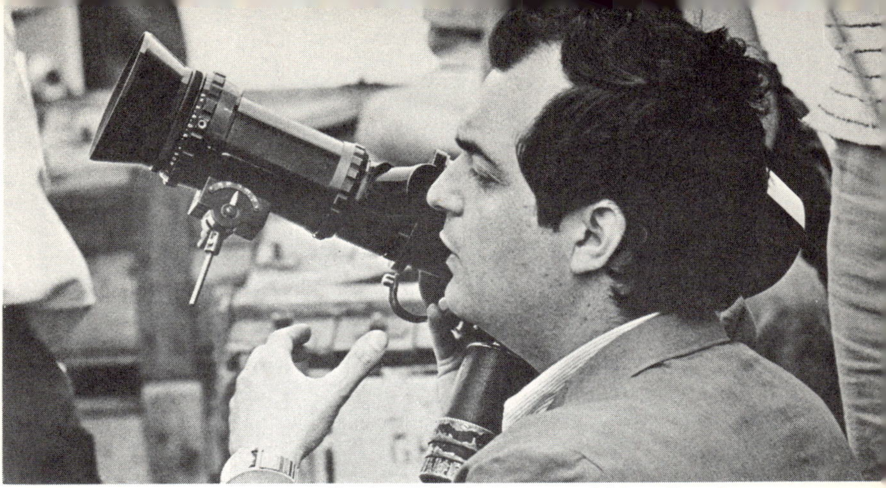

Stanley Kubrick. Courtesy of Marc Gervais.

name of scientific inquiry. . . . Thus jaded and discontented, our insatiably curious spectators will then demand instead the most diabolically candid camera yet devised by depraved man in his quest for utter, ignoble realism.

There will be increasingly ambitious attempts to combine reality with illusion. The lines between reality and illusion, amateurism and professionalism, camp and conviction, will become blurred and indistinct. Patterns of production, distribution, and exhibition will become increasingly improvisational as audiences break apart into warring, noncommunicating factions. Indeed, the relatively unified moviegoing coalition we have known for the first sixty years of the medium's history may be coming unglued already. The college 16-millimeter circuit, to take but one current example, may be setting the stage for an ever-growing audience of self-conscious aesthetes who will eventually be unable to participate in the moviegoing experience without a full complement of program notes, introductory lectures, and post-screening seminars. At this extreme of polarization, movies won't even be called movies any more, but cinemah or filluhm (as in Philharmonic Hall).

Tomorrow's movie

As for the conditions of viewing films, it is not certain that we shall ever attain for the viewer the voluptuous passivity envisaged decades ago by Aldous Huxley in *Brave New World*. As of 1970, movie audiences are still confined to the two basic senses involved with sight and sound. A few isolated experiments with "smellies" back in the '50's ended as ludicrous fiascoes, and it is unlikely any entrepreneur will ever again undertake to squirt jets of perfume out of the spectator's seat for olfactory "atmosphere." Nothing in the way of gastronomic stimulation for the movie audiences has ever passed the primal popcorn phase, and, as for Aldous Huxley's "feelies," let us say simply that the more avant-garde theatre companies, with their innovations in group-grope and confrontational contact, seem to have made the movie medium seem relatively remote and abstract in the realm of tactile sensations. All things considered, it is unlikely that the cinema will ever match the theatre, particularly the physically revolutionary theatre in the direct bodily stimulation of its audience. It doesn't follow that because some device is technically feasible, it will ever be commercially or culturally feasible, and short of an incredibly decadent transformation of movie palaces into one-man masturbation chambers, it is unlikely that Aldous Huxley's "feelies" will ever see the light of darkness.

A more interesting probe into the future may be provided by the do-it-yourself movies pioneered by Czechoslovakian film theoreticians in special movie-carnival situations. This particular do-it-yourself device invites the assembled viewers to choose one of several plot developments for the characters shown on the screen, a simple plurality of viewers being sufficient to twist the plot hither and yon. The possible variations and refinements of this device seem truly inexhaustible.

Finally, and most gratifyingly, film will be treated at long last as one of the fine arts, if not the finest. The Russians have already developed a system of visual tapes that can be projected on television, said tapes serving, therefore, the library functions of books and record albums. If rights could be cleared, and precious prints preserved, our entire cinematic heritage could be made available to students of the future. A film student could wake up in the middle of the night with sudden insight on Buster Keaton's classic silent comedies, go into his private film library and project Keaton's films, then repair to the bookshelf and take down the writings of Samuel Beckett, and compare the absurdist visions of these two remarkable artists, whose paths once actually crossed in a film called too starkly, too simply, too pretentiously *Film*. But their paths did cross, and they *are* artistically comparable, though only at some future time will it be possible to establish the validity of the comparison at a moment's scholarly notice. And at that time, people will be shooting films as casually as they type today, and a few of the film-shooters will be artists, and the rest will be what Truman Capote calls untalented writers: typists. I can't believe in my most morbid musings that there will ever come a time when beauty, truth, and personal feeling disappear completely from the screen.

ANDREW SARRIS

The cinema is a director's medium,
and if one feels that there is
something one wishes to say,
some plea one wishes to make,
then the only way to achieve it,
with any degree of satisfaction,
is by directing yourself.

RICHARD ATTENBOROUGH

Alfred Hitchcock. Courtesy of Marc Gervais.